LOW-FAT BAKING
FOR EVERY DAY

LOW-FAT BAKING FOR EVERY DAY

Over 100 delicious, low-fat recipes for cakes, bakes, cookies, bars, buns and breads, shown in 585 step-by-step photographs

Consultant Editor: **Linda Fraser**

southwater

This edition is published by Southwater,
an imprint of Anness Publishing Ltd,
Blaby Road, Wigston, Leicestershire LE18 4SE;
info@anness.com

www.southwaterbooks.com; www.annesspublishing.com

© Anness Publishing Ltd 2012

If you like the images in this book and would like to investigate
using them for publishing, promotions or advertising, please visit
our website www.practicalpictures.com for more information.

Publisher: Joanna Lorenz
Editor: Linda Fraser
Production Controller: Christine Ni

ETHICAL TRADING POLICY
At Anness Publishing we believe that business should be conducted in an
ethical and ecologically sustainable way, with respect for the environment and a
proper regard to the replacement of the natural resources we employ. As a
publisher, we use a lot of wood pulp to make high-quality paper for printing, and
that wood commonly comes from spruce trees. We are therefore currently
growing more than 750,000 trees in three Scottish forest plantations:
Berrymoss (130 hectares/320 acres), West Touxhill (125 hectares/305 acres)
and Deveron Forest (75 hectares/185 acres). The forests we manage contain more
than 3.5 times the number of trees employed each year in making paper for the
books we manufacture. Because of this ongoing ecological investment programme,
you, as our customer, can have the pleasure and reassurance of knowing that a
tree is being cultivated on your behalf to naturally replace the materials used to
make the book you are holding. Our forestry programme is run in accordance with
the UK Woodland Assurance Scheme (UKWAS) and will be certified by the
internationally recognized Forest Stewardship Council (FSC).
The FSC is a non-government organization dedicated to promoting responsible
management of the world's forests. Certification ensures forests are managed in
an environmentally sustainable and socially responsible way. For further
information about this scheme, go to www.annesspublishing.com/trees

PUBLISHER'S NOTE
Although the advice and information in this book are believed to be accurate and
true at the time of going to press, neither the authors nor the publisher can accept
any legal responsibility or liability for any errors or omissions that may be made
nor for any inaccuracies nor for any loss, harm or injury that comes about from
following instructions or advice in this book.

Previously published as part of a larger volume,
The Ultimate Low Fat Baking Book

CONTENTS

Introduction **6**

Fat and health **8**

Reducing fat in baking **9**

Low-fat alternatives **10**

Equipment **12**

Cold desserts 14

Hot desserts 28

Cakes 48

Cookies, bars and buns 68

Tea breads 80

Savoury bakes 108

Breads 136

Index **160**

Introduction

Some of us have been advised to cut down on fat, while others choose to limit their fat intake because they want a healthier lifestyle. However, fat should not be entirely excluded from our food, and most of us are aware that there are good and bad fats, so rather than cut out fat completely, we should aim rather to replace the unhealthy fats with low-fat alternatives. This has become increasingly easy for those who enjoy baking because there is now a variety of low-fat or reduced-fat products that can be used to replace full-fat versions so that you can continue to enjoy the results of your baking sessions.

Some simple tips can help you reduce fat in baking. As a general rule, choose liquid oil rather than solid fats. Select monounsaturated fats such as rapeseed oil or olive oil, and lower overall fat content by topping tarts and pies with filo pastry rather than normal pastry. Flavour in the form of salsas and herbs can be added to savoury recipes, while fruits and spices make a good substitute for sugar in sweet recipes. Low-fat yogurt or buttermilk can be used to replace some of the fat in cakes and bakes, and apple sauce is also sometimes used. For cake fillings and cheesecakes, reduced-fat or low-fat cream cheese make a delicious replacement to full-fat cream. If you really need to use hard cheese, select a strongly-flavoured Parmesan, Pecorino or Manchego, since a small amount will provide maximum flavour. If you can't use oil for your baking, a polyunsaturated margarine may be the best choice since very low-fat spreads contain too much water, and the result will not be perfect.

Be prepared by stocking up your storecupboard and refrigerator with suitable low-fat ingredients so that you can make baked treats every day of the week.

Left: This low fat version of coffee sponge drops is made even more delicious with a filling of low-fat soft cheese spiked with chopped stem ginger.

Fat and health

A suitable balance of saturated, monounsaturated and polyunsaturated fats, found in various oils, is now believed to be best for a healthy heart and well-being. A mixed-fat diet can help to promote a good proportion of desirable lipoproteins, which lower the risk of heart disease.

All fats in foods are made from the building blocks of fatty acids and glycerol, and their properties vary according to each combination.

Two types of fat are found in food – saturated and unsaturated. The unsaturated group is further divided into two types – polyunsaturated and monounsaturated fats.

A combination of the three types of fat (saturated, polyunsaturated and monounsaturated fats) are found naturally in most foods, but the amount of each type varies greatly from one food to another.

SATURATED FATS

Fatty acids are made from chains of carbon atoms. Each atom has one or more so-called free 'bonds' that link with other atoms; in this way the fatty acids transport nutrients to cells in the body. Without these free 'bonds' the carbon atom cannot form any links; it is completely 'saturated'. As a result, the body finds it difficult to process the fatty acid into energy, consequently it is stored by the body as fat.

Saturated fats should be eaten sparingly, because they can increase the level of cholesterol in the blood, which in turn can increase the risk of developing heart disease.

The main sources of saturated fats are animal products, such as meat, and butter and lard, which are solid at room temperature. However, there are also saturated fats of vegetable origin – such as coconut and palm oils, and some hard margarines and oils, which are processed by changing some of the unsaturated fatty acids to saturated ones – these are labelled 'hydrogenated vegetable oil' and should be avoided. These fats are present in many ready-made foods.

POLYUNSATURATED FATS

There are two types of polyunsaturated fats: those of vegetable or plant origin (omega 6), such as sunflower oil, soft margarine and seeds; and those from oily fish (omega 3), such as herring, mackerel and sardines. Both fats are usually liquid at room temperature. Small quantities of polyunsaturated fats are essential for good health and may help reduce cholesterol levels.

MONOUNSATURATED FATS

Found in foods such as olive oil, rapeseed oil, some nuts such as almonds and hazelnuts, oily fish and avocados, monounsaturated fats are known as good fats. This is because when eaten in moderation, they are believed to lower the blood cholesterol level. This quality may be the explanation of the low incidence of heart disease in some Mediterranean countries.

CUTTING DOWN FATS

When making your own cakes, scones, breads, cookies and muffins, it is fairly easy to cut down on obvious sources of fat in the diet, such as butter, oils, margarine, cream, whole milk and full-fat cheese, by substituting healthier ingredients, and switching to low-fat alternatives.

By being aware of foods that are high in fats and particularly in saturated fats, and by making simple changes when you are cooking, you can still supply your body with all the nutrients it needs for optimum health, while reducing the total fat content of your diet quite considerably.

Above: *Peanut oil is ideal for baking; it is low in saturated fat and free from cholesterol.*

Above: *Flax seed oil is one of the richest sources of omega-3 fatty acids.*

Above: *Pumpkin oil is high in phytosterols and helps to lower cholesterol levels.*

Reducing fat in baking

There are many simple ways of cutting down the amount of fat you use in baking. Saturated fats such as butter or lard can be replaced by unsaturated alternatives, such as vegetable oils, and nonstick cookware and baking parchment also help keep fat levels to a minimum.

Some low-fat or reduced-fat ingredients and products work better than others in cooking, but often a simple substitution of one for another works perfectly.

Instead of butter, margarine and hard fats, use low-fat spread or polyunsaturated margarine. However, very low-fat spreads with a fat content of 20% or less have a high water content and so are unsuitable for baking because, unlike butter, they will not make a cake with a light and airy texture.

If a recipe calls for full-fat products such as whole milk, cream, butter, hard margarine, crème fraîche, whole milk yogurts and hard cheese, substitute semi-skimmed or skimmed milk and milk products, low-fat yogurts, low-fat fromage frais and low-fat soft cheeses, reduced-fat hard cheeses such as Cheddar, and reduced-fat creams and crème fraîche.

For scones or pastries, avoid hard cooking fats, such as lard or hard (hydrogenated) margarine; choose the healthier option of polyunsaturated or monounsaturated oils, such as olive, sunflower or corn oil, instead. Rather than using full-fat milk, cream or yogurt, try

alternative fat-free or low-fat ingredients for all your baking and cooking. Choose fruit juice, low-fat or fat-free stock, wine or even beer to add flavour without adding any fat.

Above: For baking, choose oils that are low in saturated fats and rich in monounsaturated fats. Rapeseed (canola) oil, macadamia nut oil, flaxseed oil and walnut oil have different flavours, and are all good for baking.

Above: Beer or wine can be used instead of full-fat milk; the alcohol evaporates during cooking.

Above: Flavour can be added in baking using ingredients such as herb chutneys and olives.

Above: For savoury bakes, a tasty stock adds flavour without adding any fat.

Low-fat alternatives

Ensure that your cakes and teabreads don't stick by lining the tin with baking parchment.
Use low-fat margarine or oil to grease the tin lightly if necessary.

OIL AND FAT ALTERNATIVES

Low-fat spreads are ideal for spreading on breads and teabreads, but are unfortunately not suitable for baking because they have a high water content.

When you are baking, try to avoid saturated fats such as butter and hard margarine and use oils high in polyunsaturates such as sunflower, corn or safflower oil. When margarine is essential, choose a variety that is high in polyunsaturates.

Low-fat spread, rich buttermilk blend
Made with a high proportion of buttermilk, which is naturally low in fat. Unsuitable for baking.

Olive oil
Use this mono-unsaturated oil when a recipe requires a good strong flavour. It is best to use extra virgin olive oil.

Olive oil reduced-fat spread
Based on olive oil, this spread has a better flavour than some other low-fat spreads, but is not suitable for baking.

Reduced-fat butter
This contains about 40% fat; the rest is water and milk solids emulsified together. It is not suitable for baking.

Sunflower light
Not suitable for baking as it contains only 40% fat, plus emulsified water and milk solids.

Sunflower oil
High in polyunsaturates, this is the oil used most frequently in this book as it has a pleasant but not too dominant flavour.

Very low-fat spread
Contains only 20–30% fat and so is not suitable for baking.

LOW-FAT CHEESES

Many low-fat cheeses can be used in baking. Harder cheeses usually have a higher fat content than soft cheeses. Choose mature (sharp) cheese if possible as you need less of it to give a good flavour.

Cottage cheese
A low-fat soft cheese that is also available in a half-fat form.

Curd (farmers') cheese
This is a low-fat soft cheese made with either skimmed or semi-skimmed milk and can be used instead of cream cheese.

Edam and Maasdam
Medium-fat hard cheeses good for baking.

Feta cheese
This is a medium-fat cheese with a firm, crumbly texture. It has a slightly sour, salty flavour ranging from bland to strong.

Half-fat Cheddar and Red Leicester
These contain about 14% fat.

Mozzarella light
This is a medium-fat version of an Italian soft cheese.

Quark
Made from fermented skimmed milk, this soft, unripened white cheese has a similar flavour to soured cream. Quark is virtually free of fat.

CREAM ALTERNATIVES

Yogurt and fromage frais are good mixed with honey or liqueurs and make delicious fillings or toppings for cakes and bakes.

Bio yogurt
Bio yogurt has a mild, sweet taste.

Crème fraîche
This thick soured cream has a mild taste. Look out for half-fat crème fraîche which has a fat content of 15%.

Fromage frais
This is a soft cheese available in two grades: virtually fat free (0.4% fat), and a more creamy variety (7.9% fat).

Greek (US strained plain) yogurt
A low-fat version of this thick, creamy yogurt is available.

olive oil

sunflower oil

buttermilk blend

sunflower light

very low-fat spread

olive oil reduced-fat spread

reduced-fat butter

Left: *Try to avoid using saturated fats such as butter and margarine. Instead use oils or spreads high in polyunsaturates.*

Above: There are a whole range of lower-fat cheeses that can be used in baking.

Left: Use low-fat milks for baking, and try yogurt or fromage frais as an alternative to cream. Eggs are essential for baking; the yolks create a fine texture and act as an emulsifier, while the whites add structure in baking.

LOW-FAT MILKS

Buttermilk
Made from skimmed milk with a bacterial culture added, it is very low in fat.

Powdered skimmed milk
A useful, low-fat standby.

Semi-skimmed milk
With a fat content of only 1.5–1.8%, this milk tastes less rich than full-cream milk. It is favoured by many people for everyday use for precisely this reason.

Skimmed milk
This milk has had virtually all the fat removed leaving only 0.1–0.3%. It is ideal for those wishing to cut down their fat intake.

Equipment

If you choose good quality, heavy non-stick cookware, the amount of fat used in baking can be kept to an absolute minimum.

Baking parchment
For lining tins and baking sheets to ensure cakes, meringues and biscuits do not stick.

Baking sheet
Choose a large, heavy baking sheet that will not warp at high temperatures.

Balloon whisk
Perfect for whisking egg whites and incorporating air into other light mixtures.

Box grater
This multi-purpose grater can be used for citrus rind, fruit and vegetables, and cheese.

Brown paper
Used for wrapping around the outside of cake tins (pans) to protect the cake mixture from the full heat of the oven.

Cake tester
A simple implement that, when inserted into a cooked cake, will come out clean if the cake is ready.

Cook's knife
This heavy, wide blade is ideal for chopping.

Deep round cake tin (pan)
This deep tin is ideal for baking fruit cakes.

Elecric whisk
Ideal for creaming cake mixtures, whipping cream and whisking egg whites.

Honey twirl
For spooning honey without making a mess.

Juicer
Made from porcelain, glass or plastic – used for squeezing the juice from citrus fruits.

Loaf tin (pan)
Available in various sizes and used for making loaf-shaped breads and teabreads.

Measuring jug (cup)
Absolutely essential for measuring any kind of liquid accurately.

Measuring spoons
Standard measuring spoons are essential for measuring small quantities of ingredients.

Mixing bowls
A set of different sized bowls is essential in any kitchen for whisking and mixing.

Muffin tin (pan)
Shaped into individual cups, this tin is much simpler to use than individual paper cases. It can also be used for baking small pies and tarts.

Nutmeg grater
This miniature grater is used for grating whole nutmegs.

Nylon sieve
Suitable for most baking purposes, and particularly for sieving foods that react adversely with metal.

Palette knife (metal spatula)
This implement is needed for loosening pies, tarts and breads from baking sheets and for smoothing icing over cakes.

Pastry brush
Useful for brushing excess flour from pastry and brushing glazes over pastries, breads and tarts.

Pastry (cookie) cutters
A variety of shapes and sizes of cutter is useful when stamping out pastry, biscuits and scones.

Rectangular cake tin (pan)
For making tray cakes and bakes, served cut into slices.

Ring mould
Perfect for making angel cakes and other ring-shaped cakes.

Sandwich cake tin (pan)
Ideal for sponge cakes; it is very useful to have two of them.

Scissors
Vital for cutting paper and snipping dough and pastry.

Square cake tin (pan)
Used for making square cakes or cakes served cut into smaller squares.

Swiss roll tin (jelly roll pan)
This shallow tin is designed especially for Swiss rolls.

Vegetable knife
A useful knife for preparing the fruit and vegetables that you may add to your bakes.

Wire rack
Ideal for cooling cakes and bakes, allowing the circulation of air, and prevent sogginess.

Wire sieve
A large wire sieve is ideal for most normal baking purposes.

Wooden spoon
Essential for mixing ingredients and creaming mixtures.

Right: *Invest in a few useful items for easy low-fat cooking: non-stick cookware and accurate measuring equipment are essential for good results.*

electric

square cake tin

loaf tin

rectangular cake tin

baking sheet

wooden spoon

cook's knife

balloon whisk

mixing bowls

baking parchment

scissors

brown paper

vegetable knife

sandwich cake tin

ring mould

honey twirl

measuring jug

wire rack

pastry cutters

deep round cake tin

wire rack

pastry brush

juicer

Swiss roll tin

nutmeg grater

box grater

measuring spoons

wire sieve

nylon sieve

muffin tin

COLD DESSERTS

These desserts look so yummy that you would never believe they were low in fat. In fact they are all made with reduced-fat ingredients – and they taste every bit as good as their full-fat creamy counterparts. You need never refuse a sweet treat again.

Chestnut and Orange Roulade

This deliciously moist cake, which has a delightful tangy flavour, is ideal to serve as a dessert or it would be perfect for a special teatime treat.

SERVES 8

3 eggs, separated
115g/4oz/generous ½ cup caster (superfine) sugar
225g/8oz/1 cup canned unsweetened chestnut purée
grated rind and juice of 1 orange
icing (confectioners') sugar, for dusting

For the filling

225g/8oz/1 cup low-fat soft (farmer's) cheese
15ml/1 tbsp clear honey
1 orange

1 Preheat the oven to 180°C/350°/Gas 4. Grease a 30 x 20cm/12 x 8in Swiss roll tin (jelly roll pan) and line with baking parchment. Whisk the egg yolks and sugar until thick and creamy.

2 Put the chestnut purée in a separate bowl. Whisk in the orange rind and juice, then whisk the flavoured chestnut purée into the egg mixture.

3 Whisk the egg whites until fairly stiff. Using a metal spoon, stir a spoonful of the egg into the chestnut mixture to lighten it. Fold in the rest. Spoon into the prepared tin and bake for 30 minutes. Cool for 5 minutes, then cover until cold.

4 Meanwhile, make the filling. Put the soft cheese in a bowl with the honey. Finely grate the orange rind and add to the bowl. Peel away all the pith from the orange, cut the fruit into segments, chop roughly and set aside. Add any juice to the cheese mixture, then beat until it is smooth. Mix in the chopped orange.

5 Dust a sheet of baking parchment thickly with icing sugar. Carefully turn the roulade out on to the paper, then peel off the lining paper. Spread the filling over the roulade and roll up like a Swiss (jelly) roll. Transfer to a plate and dust with some more icing sugar.

Cook's Tip

Do not whisk the egg whites too stiffly, or it will be difficult to fold them into the mixture and they will form lumps in the roulade.

Nutritional information

Calories	185kcal775kj
Fat	4g
Saturated fat	1.5g
Cholesterol	76mg
Fibre	1.4g

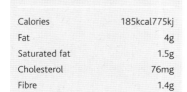

Snowballs

A variation on the basic meringue recipe, these snowballs are made with cornflour. They make an excellent accompaniment to ice cream.

2 Add the sugar, whisking until the meringue is very stiff. Whisk in the cornflour, vinegar and vanilla essence.

3 Spoon small mounds of the mixture on to the prepared baking sheets.

4 Remove from the oven and leave to cool on the baking sheet. When the snowballs are cold, remove them from the paper with a palette knife (metal spatula).

Makes about 20

2 egg whites
115g/4oz/generous ½ cup caster (superfine) sugar
15ml/1 tbsp cornflour (cornstarch), sifted
5ml/1 tsp white wine vinegar
1.5ml/¼ tsp vanilla essence (extract)

Nutritional information

Calories	29kcal/124kj
Fat	0.01g
Saturated fat	0g
Cholesterol	0mg
Fibre	0g

1 Preheat the oven to 150°C/300°F/ Gas 2. Line two baking sheets with baking parchment. Whisk the egg whites in a grease-free bowl until stiff, using an electric whisk.

Muscovado Meringues

These light brown meringues are extremely low in fat and are delicious served on their own or sandwiched together with a fresh fruit soft cheese filling.

MAKES ABOUT 20

115g/4oz/¹⁄₂ cup light muscovado (brown) sugar

2 egg whites

5ml/1 tsp finely chopped walnuts

Nutritional information

Calories	197kcal/826kj
Fat	6.8g
Saturated fat	1.4g
Cholesterol	25mg
Fibre	0.7g

1 Preheat the oven to 160°C/325°F/ Gas 3. Line two baking sheets with baking parchment. Press the sugar through a metal sieve into a bowl.

4 Sprinkle the meringues with the walnuts. Bake for 30 minutes. Cool for 5 minutes on the baking sheets, then leave on a wire rack.

2 Whisk the egg whites in a clean, dry bowl, until very stiff and dry, whisk in the sugar, 15ml/1 tbsp at a time, until the meringue is thick and glossy.

3 Spoon small mounds of the mixture on to the prepared baking sheets.

Raspberry Vacherin

Meringue rounds filled with orange-flavoured fromage frais and fresh raspberries
makes a perfect dinner party dessert.

SERVES 6

3 egg whites
175g/6oz/scant 1 cup caster
    (superfine) sugar
5ml/1 tsp chopped almonds
icing (confectioners') sugar, for dusting
raspberry leaves, to decorate (optional)

For the filling

175g/6oz/³⁄₄ cup low-fat soft
    (farmer's) cheese
15–30ml/1–2 tbsp clear honey
15ml/1 tbsp Cointreau
120ml/4 fl oz/¹⁄₂ cup low-fat fromage
    frais or low-fat crème fraîche
225g/8oz/1¹⁄₄ cup raspberries

Cook's Tip

Before whisking the egg whites, make sure
that the bowl you use is perfectly clean
and free of any oil, otherwise they will
not become stiff. When making the
meringue, a good test is to whisk the egg
whites until they are so stiff that you can
turn the bowl upside down without them
falling out.

Nutritional information	
Calories	248kcal/1041kj
Fat	2.2g
Saturated fat	0.8g
Cholesterol	4mg
Fibre	1.1g

1 Preheat the oven to 140°C/275°F/
Gas 1. Draw a 20cm/8in circle on
two pieces of baking parchment. Turn the
paper over so the marking is on the
underside and use it to line two heavy
baking sheets.

2 Whisk the egg whites in a grease-free
bowl until very stiff, then gradually
whisk in the caster sugar to make a stiff
meringue mixture.

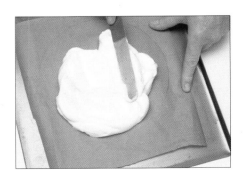

3 Spoon the mixture on to the circles
on the prepared baking sheets,
spreading the meringue evenly to the
edges. Sprinkle one meringue round with
the chopped almonds.

4 Bake for 1¹⁄₂–2 hours, then lift the
meringue rounds off the baking
sheets, peel away the paper and cool.

5 To make the filling, cream the soft
cheese with the honey and liqueur in
a bowl. Fold in the fromage frais and
raspberries, reserving three for decoration.

6 Place the plain meringue round on a
board, spread with the filling and top
with the nut-covered round. Dust the top
with icing sugar, transfer to a serving
plate and decorate with the reserved
raspberries, and a sprig of raspberry
leaves, if you like.

Strawberry Gâteau

It's hard to believe that this delicious gâteau is low in fat, but it's true, so enjoy!

SERVES 6

2 eggs
75g/3oz/scant ½ cup caster
     (superfine) sugar
grated rind of ½ orange
50g/2oz/½ cup plain
     (all-purpose) flour
icing (confectioners') sugar, for dusting
strawberry leaves, to decorate (optional)

For the filling

275g/10oz/1¼ cups low-fat
     soft (farmer's) cheese
grated rind of ½ orange
30ml/2 tbsp caster (superfine) sugar
60ml/4 tbsp low-fat fromage frais or
     low-fat crème fraîche
225g/8oz/2 cups strawberries, halved
25g/1oz/2 tbsp chopped
     almonds, toasted

Variation

Use other soft fruits in season, such as currants, raspberries, blackberries or blueberries, or try a mixture of a few different berries.

Nutritional information

Calories	213kcal/893kj
Fat	6.1g
Saturated fat	1.8g
Cholesterol	70mg
Fibre	1g

1 Preheat the oven to 190°C/375°F/ Gas 5. Grease a 30 x 20cm/12 x 8in Swiss roll tin (jelly roll pan) and line with baking parchment.

2 In a bowl, whisk the eggs, sugar and orange rind together with a hand-held electric whisk until thick and mousse-like (when the whisk is lifted, a trail should remain on the surface of the mixture for at least 15 seconds).

3 Fold in the flour with a metal spoon. Turn into the prepared tin. Bake for 15–20 minutes, or until the cake springs back when pressed. Turn the cake on to a wire rack, remove the lining paper and cool.

4 Meanwhile make the filling. In a bowl, mix the soft cheese with the orange rind, sugar and fromage frais until smooth. Divide between two bowls. Chop half the strawberry halves and add to one bowl of filling.

5 Cut the sponge into three equal pieces and sandwich together with the strawberry filling. Spread two-thirds of the plain filling over the sides of the cake and press on the toasted almonds.

6 Spread the rest of the filling on the top of the cake and add strawberry halves, and leaves if you like. Dust with icing sugar and transfer to a serving plate.

Mixed Berry Tart

The orange-flavoured pastry in this tart is delicious with the fresh fruits of summer.
Serve this with some extra shreds of orange rind scattered on top.

SERVES 8

For the pastry
225g/8oz/2 cups plain
   (all-purpose) flour
115g/4oz/½ cup unsalted butter
finely grated rind of 1 orange, plus
extra to decorate

For the filling
300ml/½ pint/1¼ cups crème fraîche
finely grated rind of 1 lemon
10ml/2 tsp icing (confectioners') sugar
675g/1½lb/6 cups mixed
   summer berries

1 To make the pastry, put the flour and butter in a large bowl. Using your fingertips, rub in the butter until the mixture resembles crumbs.

2 Add the orange rind and enough cold water to make a soft dough.

4 Line a 23cm/9in loose-based flan tin (tart pan) with the pastry. Chill for 30 minutes. Preheat the oven to 200°C/400°F/Gas 6 and place a baking sheet in the oven to heat up.

5 Weight the pastry base with baking parchment and baking beans and bake blind on the baking sheet for 15 minutes. Remove the paper and beans and bake the pastry for about 10 minutes, until it is golden. Allow to cool.

6 To make the filling, whisk the crème fraîche, lemon rind and sugar together and pour into the pastry case (pie crust). Top with fruit, sprinkle with orange rind, and serve, sliced.

Variation

For a tangier tart, substitute the finely grated rind of a lemon for that of an orange when making the pastry. Sprinkle the finished tart with lemon rind instead of orange rind.

3 Roll into a ball and chill for at least 20 minutes. Roll out the pastry on a lightly floured surface until it is large enough to line the flan tin.

Nutritional information	
Calories	293kcal/1223kj
Fat	18g
Saturated fat	5.9g
Cholesterol	40mg
Fibre	2.4g

Blueberry and Orange Baskets

Impress your guests with these pretty, fruit-filled crêpes. When blueberries are out of season, replace them with other soft fruit, such as raspberries.

SERVES 6

For the pancakes

150g/5oz/1¼ cups plain (all-purpose) flour
pinch of salt
2 egg whites
200ml/7fl oz/scant 1 cup skimmed milk
150ml/¼ pint/⅔ cup orange juice

For the filling

4 medium-size oranges
225g/8oz/2 cups blueberries

1 Preheat the oven to 200°C/400°F/ Gas 6. To make the pancakes, sift the flour and salt into a bowl. Make a well in the centre of the flour and add the egg whites, milk and orange juice. Whisk until the batter is smooth and bubbly.

2 Lightly grease a heavy or non-stick pancake pan and heat until it is very hot. Pour in just enough batter to cover the base of the pan, swirling it so that you cover the pan evenly.

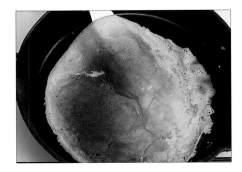

3 Cook until the pancake has set and is golden, and then turn it to cook the other side. Remove the pancake to a sheet of kitchen paper, and then cook the remaining batter, to make 6–8 pancakes.

4 Place six small ovenproof bowls or moulds on a baking sheet and arrange the pancakes over these. Bake the pancakes in the oven for about 10 minutes, until they are crisp and set into the shape of the moulds. Carefully lift the "baskets" off the moulds and set aside until completely cool.

5 For the filling, pare a thin piece of orange rind from one orange and cut it into fine strips. Blanch the strips in boiling water for 30 seconds, rinse in cold water and set aside. Cut all the peel and white pith from all the oranges.

6 Divide the oranges into segments, catching the juice, mix with the blueberries and warm gently. Spoon the fruit into the baskets and sprinkle with shreds of rind.

Cook's Tip

Don't fill the pancake baskets until you are ready to serve them, because they will absorb the fruit juice and begin to soften.

Nutritional information

Calories	159kcal/673kj
Fat	0.5g
Saturated fat	0.1g
Cholesterol	1mg
Fibre	3.3g

HOT DESSERTS

Heartwarming hot puddings with fruity ingredients are
perfect to round off a satisfying meal. And you can eat
them without guilt, because they are all low in fat
and cholesterol.

Filo and Apricot Purses

Filo pastry is very easy to use and is low in fat. Keep a packet in the freezer ready for rustling up a speedy tea-time treat.

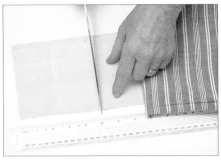

2 Cut the filo pastry into twenty-four 13cm/5in squares, pile the squares on top of each other and cover with a clean dishtowel to prevent the pastry from drying out and becoming brittle.

3 Lay a pastry square on a flat surface, brush lightly with melted margarine and lay another square diagonally on top. Brush the top square with margarine. Spoon a small mound of apricot mixture in the centre of the pastry, bring up the edges and pinch together in a money-bag shape. Make 12 purses in all.

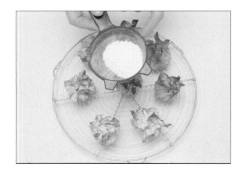

4 Arrange the purses on the prepared baking sheets and bake for 5–8 minutes until golden. Transfer to a wire rack, dust with icing sugar. Serve warm.

MAKES 12

115g/4oz/½ cup ready-to-eat dried apricots
45ml/3 tbsp apricot compote or conserve
3 amaretti, crushed
3 sheets filo pastry, thawed if frozen
20ml/4 tsp soft margarine, melted
icing (confectioners') sugar, for dusting

1 Preheat the oven to 180°C/350°F/ Gas 4. Grease two baking sheets. Chop the apricots, put them in a bowl and stir in the apricot compote. Add the crushed amaretti and mix well.

Nutritional information

Calories	58kcal/245kj
Fat	1.9g
Saturated fat	0.4g
Cholesterol	.12mg
Fibre	0.7g

Filo Scrunchies

Quick and easy to make, these pastries are ideal to serve at tea time. Eat them warm or they will lose their crispness.

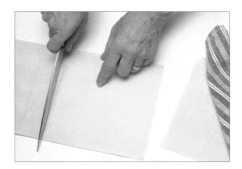

MAKES 6

5 apricots or plums
4 sheets filo pastry, thawed if frozen
20ml/4 tsp soft margarine, melted
50g/2oz/1/4 cup demerara (raw) sugar
30ml/2 tbsp flaked (sliced) almonds
icing (confectioners') sugar, for dusting

1 Preheat the oven to 190°C/375°F/ Gas 5. Halve the apricots or plums, remove the stones (pits) and slice the fruit. Cut the filo pastry into twelve 18cm/7in squares. Pile the squares on top of each other and cover with a clean dishtowel to prevent the pastry from drying out.

4 Place the scrunchies on a baking sheet. Bake for 8–10 minutes until golden brown, then loosen the scrunchies from the baking sheet with a metal spatula and transfer to a wire rack. Dust with icing sugar and serve at once.

Nutritional information

Calories	132kcal/555kj
Fat	4.2g
Saturated fat	0.6g
Cholesterol	0mg
Fibre	0.7g

2 Remove one square of filo and brush it with melted margarine. Lay a second filo square on top, then, using your fingers, mould the pastry into folds. Make five more scrunchies, working quickly so that the pastry does not dry out.

3 Arrange a few slices of fruit in the folds of each scrunchie, then sprinkle generously with the demerara sugar and flaked almonds.

Plum Filo Pockets

These attractive party parcels are high in fibre as well as being a tasty treat.

SERVES 4

115g/4oz/½ cup skimmed-milk
   soft (farmer's) cheese
15ml/1 tbsp light muscovado
   (brown) sugar
2.5ml/½ tsp ground cloves
8 large, firm plums, halved and stoned
8 sheets filo pastry, thawed if frozen
sunflower oil, for brushing
icing (confectioners') sugar, to sprinkle

Nutritional information

Calories	188kcal/790kj
Fat	1.9g
Saturated fat	0.3g
Cholesterol	0.3mg
Fibre	2.6g

1 Preheat the oven to 220°C/425°F/ Gas 7. Mix together the cheese, sugar and cloves.

2 Sandwich the plum halves back together with a spoonful of the cheese mixture in each plum.

3 Spread out the pastry and cut into 16 pieces, about 23cm/9in square. Brush one lightly with oil and place a second at a diagonal on top. Repeat with the remaining squares.

4 Place a plum on each pastry square, and gather the corners together. Place on a baking sheet. Bake for 15–18 minutes, until golden, then dust with icing sugar.

Apple Couscous Pudding

This unusual mixture makes a delicious family pudding with a rich, fruity flavour, but virtually no fat.

1 Preheat the oven to 200°C/400°F/ Gas 6. Place the apple juice, couscous, sultanas and spice in a pan and bring to the boil, stirring. Cover and simmer for 10–12 minutes, until all the free liquid has been absorbed.

2 Peel, core and slice the apple. Spoon half the couscous mixture into a 1.2 litre/2 pint/5 cup ovenproof dish and top with half the apple slices. Top with the remaining couscous.

3 Arrange the remaining apple slices overlapping on top and sprinkle with demerara sugar. Bake for 25–30 minutes, or until golden brown. Serve hot, with low-fat yogurt.

SERVES 4

600ml/1 pint/2½ cups apple juice
115g/4oz/²⁄₃ cup couscous
40g/1½ oz/3 tbsp sultanas
   (golden raisins)
2.5ml/½ tsp mixed (apple pie) spice
1 large cooking apple
30ml/2 tbsp demerara (raw) sugar
low-fat natural (plain) yogurt, to serve

Nutritional information	
Calories	194kcal815kj
Fat	0.6g
Saturated fat	0.1g
Cholesterol	0mg
Fibre	0.8g

Mango and Amaretti Strudel

Fresh mango and crushed amaretti wrapped in wafer-thin filo pastry make a special treat that is equally good made with apricots or plums.

SERVES 4

1 large mango
grated rind of 1 lemon
2 amaretti
25g/1oz/2 tbsp demerara
    (raw) sugar
60ml/4 tbsp wholemeal
    (whole-wheat) breadcrumbs
2 sheets filo pastry, each
    48 x 28cm/19 x 11in, thawed
    if frozen
20g/³⁄₄oz/4 tsp soft
    margarine, melted
15ml/1 tbsp chopped almonds
icing (confectioners') sugar,
    for dusting

1 Preheat the oven to 190°C/375°F/ Gas 5. Lightly grease a large baking sheet. Halve, stone and peel the mango. Cut the flesh into cubes, then place them in a bowl, and sprinkle with grated lemon rind.

2 Crush the amaretti and mix them with the demerara sugar and the wholemeal breadcrumbs.

4 Sprinkle the filo with the amaretti mixture, leaving a 5cm/2in border on each long side. Arrange the mango cubes over the top.

5 Roll up the filo from one of the long sides like a Swiss roll (jelly roll). Lift the strudel on to the baking sheet with the join underneath. Brush with the remaining melted margarine and sprinkle with the chopped almonds.

Cook's Tip

The easiest way to prepare a mango is to cut horizontally through the fruit, keeping the knife blade close to the stone. Repeat on the other side of the stone and peel off the skin. Remove the remaining skin and flesh from around the stone.

3 Lay one sheet of filo on a flat surface and brush with margarine. Top with the second sheet, brush with one-third of the remaining margarine, then fold both sheets over, if necessary, to make a rectangle measuring 28 x 23cm/11 x 9in. Brush with half the remaining margarine.

6 Bake for 20–25 minutes until golden brown, then transfer to a board. Dust with the icing sugar, slice diagonally and serve warm.

Nutritional information	
Calories	239kcal/1006kj
Fat	8.5g
Saturated fat	4.4g
Cholesterol	17.3mg
Fibre	3.3g

Baked Blackberry Cheesecake

This light, low-fat cheesecake is best made with wild blackberries, if they're available, but cultivated ones will do; or substitute other soft fruit, such as loganberries, raspberries or blueberries.

SERVES 5

175g/6oz/³⁄₄ cup low-fat
    cottage cheese
150g/5oz/²⁄₃ cup low-fat natural
    (plain) yogurt
15ml/1 tbsp plain (all-purpose)
    wholemeal (whole-wheat) flour
25g/1oz/2 tbsp golden caster
    (superfine) sugar
1 egg
1 egg white
finely grated rind and juice
    of ¹⁄₂ lemon
200g/7oz/1³⁄₄ cups fresh or frozen and
    thawed blackberries

1 Preheat the oven to 180°C/350°F/ Gas 4. Lightly grease and base-line an 18cm/7in sandwich tin (pan).

2 Place the cottage cheese in a food processor and process until smooth. Alternatively, rub it though a sieve.

3 Add the yogurt, flour, sugar, egg and egg white and mix. Add the lemon rind, juice and blackberries, reserving a few for decoration.

4 Tip the mixture into the prepared tin and bake for 30–35 minutes, or until it is just set. Turn off the oven and leave for a further 30 minutes.

5 Run a knife around the edge of the cheesecake, then turn it out. Remove the lining paper and place on a warm serving plate.

6 Decorate with the reserved blackberries and serve warm.

Cook's Tip

If you prefer to use canned blackberries, choose those canned in natural juice and drain the fruit well before adding it to the cheesecake mixture. The juice can be served with the cheesecake, but this will increase the total calories.

Nutritional information

Calories	103kcal/437kj
Fat	2g
Saturated fat	0.8g
Cholesterol	41mg
Fibre	1.6g

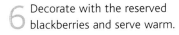
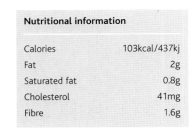

Baked Apple in Honey and Lemon

A classic mix of flavours in a healthy, traditional family pudding. Serve warm, with skimmed-milk custard.

SERVES 4

4 medium-size cooking apples
15ml/1 tbsp clear honey
grated rind and juice of 1 lemon
15ml/1 tbsp low-fat spread

Nutritional information	
Calories	651kcal/2703kj
Fat	1.7g
Saturated fat	0.4g
Cholesterol	0mg
Fibre	1.7g

1 Preheat the oven to 180°C/350°F/ Gas 4. Remove the cores from the apples, leaving them whole.

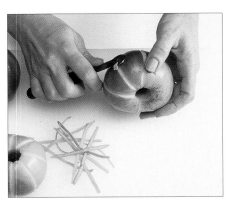

2 With a cannelle or sharp knife, cut lines through the apple skin at intervals and place in an ovenproof dish.

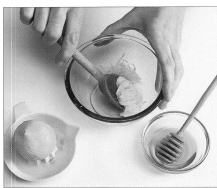

3 Mix together the honey, lemon rind, juice and low-fat spread.

4 Spoon the mixture into the apples and cover the dish with foil or a lid. Bake for 40–45 minutes, or until the apples are tender. Serve with skimmed-milk custard.

Strawberry and Apple Crumble

A high fibre, healthier version of the classic apple crumble. Raspberries can be used instead of strawberries, either fresh or frozen. Serve warm, with skimmed-milk custard.

1 Preheat the oven to 180°C/350°F/ Gas 4. Peel, core and slice the apples. Halve the strawberries.

2 Toss together the apples, strawberries, sweetener, cinnamon and orange juice. Tip into a 1.2 litre/2 pint/5 cup ovenproof dish, or four individual dishes.

3 Combine the flour and oats in a bowl and mix in the low-fat spread with a fork.

4 Sprinkle the crumble evenly over the fruit. Bake for 40–45 minutes (20–25 minutes for individual dishes), until golden brown and bubbling. Serve warm, with low-fat custard or yogurt.

SERVES 4

450g/1lb cooking apples
150g/5oz/1¼ cups
    strawberries, hulled
30ml/2 tbsp granulated sweetener
2.5ml/½ tsp ground cinnamon
30ml/2 tbsp orange juice

For the crumble

45ml/3 tbsp plain (all-purpose)
    wholemeal (whole-wheat) flour
50g/2oz/⅔ cups rolled oats
25g/1oz/2 tbsp low-fat spread

Nutritional information	
Calories	182kcal/769kj
Fat	4g
Saturated fat	0.9g
Cholesterol	0mg
Fibre	3.5g

Crunchy Gooseberry Crumble

Gooseberries are perfect for traditional family puddings like this one. When they are out of season, other fruits such as apples, plums or rhubarb could be used instead.

2 To make the crumble, place the oats, flour and oil in a bowl, and stir with a fork until evenly mixed.

3 Stir in the demerara sugar and walnuts, then spread evenly over the gooseberries. Bake for 25–30 minutes, or until golden and bubbling. Serve hot with low-fat yogurt, or custard made with skimmed milk.

SERVES 4

500g/1¼lb/5 cups gooseberries
50g/2oz/¼ cup caster
   (superfine) sugar
75g/3oz/scant 1 cup rolled oats
75g/3oz/⅔ cup plain
   (all-purpose) wholemeal
   (whole-wheat) flour
60ml/4 tbsp sunflower oil
50g/2oz/¼ cup demerara
   (raw) sugar
30ml/2 tbsp chopped walnuts
low-fat yogurt or custard, to serve

1 Preheat the oven to 200°C/400°F/ Gas 6. Place the gooseberries in a pan with the caster sugar. Cover the pan and cook over a low heat for 10 minutes, until the gooseberries are just tender. Tip into an ovenproof dish.

Cook's Tip

The best cooking gooseberries are the early small, firm green ones.

Nutritional information

Calories	422kcal/1770kj
Fat	18.5g
Saturated fat	2.3g
Cholesterol	0mg
Fibre	5.1g

Ginger Upside Down Pudding

A traditional pudding goes down well on a cold winter's day. This one is quite quick to make and looks very impressive.

1 Preheat the oven to 180°C/350°F/ Gas 4. For the topping, brush the base and sides of a 23cm/9in round spring-form cake tin (pan) with oil. Sprinkle the sugar over the base.

2 Arrange the peaches cut-side down in the tin with a walnut half in each.

3 For the base, sift together the flour, bicarbonate of soda, ginger and cinnamon, then stir in the sugar. Beat together the egg, milk and oil.

4 Mix into the dry ingredients until smooth. Pour the mixture evenly over the peaches and bake for 35–40 minutes, until firm to the touch. Turn out on to a serving plate. Serve hot with low-fat yogurt or custard.

Nutritional information

Calories	432kcal/1812kj
Fat	16.5g
Saturated fat	2.3g
Cholesterol	48mg
Fibre	4.8g

SERVES 4–6

sunflower oil, for brushing
15ml/1 tbsp soft brown sugar
4 medium peaches, halved and stoned
8 walnut halves

For the base

115g/4oz/½ cup plain (all-purpose) wholemeal (whole-wheat) flour
2.5ml/½ tsp bicarbonate of soda (baking soda)
7.5ml/1½ tsp ground ginger
5ml/1 tsp ground cinnamon
115g/4oz/½ cup dark muscovado (molasses) sugar
1 egg
120ml/4fl oz/½ cup skimmed milk
50ml/2fl oz/¼ cup sunflower oil

Latticed Peaches

An elegant dessert; it certainly doesn't look low in fat, but it really is. Use canned peach halves when fresh peaches are out of season, or if you're short of time.

SERVES 6

For the pastry
115g/4oz/1 cup plain
   (all-purpose) flour
40g/1½ oz/3 tbsp butter or
   sunflower margarine
45ml/3 tbsp low-fat natural
   (plain) yogurt
30ml/2 tbsp orange juice
skimmed milk, for glaze

For the filling
3 ripe peaches or nectarines
45ml/3 tbsp ground almonds
30ml/2 tbsp low-fat natural
   (plain) yogurt
finely grated rind of 1 small orange
1.5ml/¼ tsp natural almond
   essence (extract)

For the sauce
1 ripe peach or nectarine
45ml/3 tbsp orange juice

Cook's Tip

This dessert is best eaten fairly fresh from the oven, as the pastry can toughen slightly if left to stand. So assemble the peaches in their pastry on a baking sheet, chill in the refrigerator, and bake just before serving.

Nutritional information

Calories	219kcal/916kj
Fat	10.8g
Saturated fat	1.6g
Cholesterol	1mg
Fibre	2.4g

1 For the pastry, sift the flour into a bowl and, using your fingertips, rub in the butter or margarine evenly. Stir in the yogurt and orange juice to bind the mixture into a firm dough.

2 Roll out about half the pastry thinly and use a biscuit cutter to stamp out rounds about 7.5cm/3in in diameter, slightly larger than the circumference of the peaches. Place on a lightly greased baking sheet.

3 Skin the peaches or nectarines, halve and remove the stones. Mix together the almonds, yogurt, orange rind and almond essence. Spoon into the hollows of each peach half and place, cut-side down, on to the pastry rounds.

4 Roll out the remaining pastry thinly and cut into thin strips. Arrange the strips over the peaches to form a lattice, brushing with milk to secure firmly. Trim off the ends neatly.

5 Chill in the fridge for 30 minutes. Preheat the oven to 200°C/400°F/ Gas 6. Brush with milk and bake for 15–18 minutes, until golden brown.

6 For the sauce, skin the peach or nectarine and halve it to remove the stone. Place the flesh in a food processor, with the orange juice, and purée it until smooth. Serve the peaches hot, with the peach sauce spooned around.

Hot Plum Batter

Other fruits can be used in place of plums, depending on the season. Canned black cherries are a convenient store-cupboard substitute.

SERVES 4

450g/1lb ripe red plums,
   quartered and stoned
200ml/7fl oz/scant 1 cup skimmed milk
60ml/4 tbsp skimmed milk powder (non fat
   dry milk)
15ml/1 tbsp light muscovado
   (light brown) sugar
5ml/1 tsp vanilla essence (extract)
75g/3oz/²/₃ cup self-raising (self-rising) flour
2 egg whites
icing (confectioners') sugar, to sprinkle

Nutritional information	
Calories	195kcal/816kj
Fat	0.5g
Saturated fat	0.1g
Cholesterol	2.8mg
Fibre	2.3g

1 Preheat the oven to 220°C/425°F/ Gas 7. Lightly oil a wide, shallow ovenproof dish and add the plums.

2 Pour the milk, milk powder, sugar, vanilla, flour and egg whites into a food processor. Process until smooth.

3 Pour the batter over the plums. Bake for 25–30 minutes, or until well risen and golden. Sprinkle with icing sugar and serve immediately.

Glazed Apricot Sponge

Puddings can be very high in saturated fat, but this one uses the minimum of oil and no eggs. Other fruits could be used for this dessert, such as plums.

SERVES 4

10ml/2 tsp golden (light corn) syrup

411g/14½oz can apricot halves in fruit juice

150g/5oz/1¼ cup self-raising (self-rising) flour

75g/3oz/1½ cups fresh breadcrumbs

90g/3½oz/⅔ cup light muscovado (light brown) sugar

5ml/1 tsp ground cinnamon

30ml/2 tbsp sunflower oil

175ml/6fl oz/¾ cup skimmed milk

1 Preheat the oven to 180°C/350°F/ Gas 4. Lightly oil a 900ml/1½ pint/ 3¾ cup pudding bowl. Spoon in the syrup.

2 Drain the apricots and reserve the juice. Arrange about eight halves in the bowl. Purée the rest of the apricots with the juice and set aside.

3 Mix the flour, breadcrumbs, sugar and cinnamon, then beat in the oil and milk. Spoon into the bowl and bake for 50–55 minutes, or untilgolden. Serve with the puréed fruit as a sauce.

Nutritional information	
Calories	364kcal/1530kj
Fat	6.5g
Saturated fat	0.9g
Cholesterol	0.9mg
Fibre	2.4g

Fruity Bread Pudding

A popular family favourite pudding from grandmother's day, with a lighter healthier touch.

2 Remove the pan from the heat and stir in the bread, spice and banana. Spoon the mixture into a shallow 1.2 litre/2 pint/5 cup ovenproof dish and pour over the milk.

3 Sprinkle with demerara sugar and bake for 25–30 minutes, until firm and golden brown. Serve hot or cold with natural low-fat yogurt.

SERVES 4

75g/3oz/½ cup mixed dried fruit
150ml/¼ pint/⅔ cup apple juice
115g/4oz stale brown or white
  bread, diced
5ml/1 tsp mixed (apple pie) spice
1 large banana, sliced
150ml/¼ pint/⅔ cup skimmed milk
15ml/1 tbsp demerara (raw) sugar
low-fat natural (plain) yogurt, to serve

1 Preheat the oven to 200°C/400°F/ Gas 6. Place the dried fruit in a small pan with the apple juice and bring to the boil.

Nutritional information

Calories	190kcal/800kj
Fat	0.9g
Saturated fat	0.2g
Cholesterol	0.8mg
Fibre	1.8g

Cook's Tip

Different types of bread will absorb varying amounts of liquid, so you may need to adjust the amount of milk to allow for this.

Feather-light Peach Pudding

On chilly days, try this hot fruit pudding with its tantalizing sponge topping.

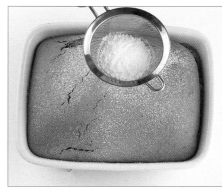

1 Preheat the oven to 180°C/350°F/ Gas 4. Drain the peaches and put into a 1 litre/1¾ pint/4 cup pie dish with 30ml/2 tbsp of the juice.

4 Lightly dust the top with icing sugar before serving hot with the custard.

SERVES 4

400g/14oz/3 cups canned peach slices in natural juice
50g/2oz/4 tbsp low-fat spread
40g/1½oz/3 tbsp soft light brown sugar
1 egg, beaten
50g/2oz/½ cup plain (all-purpose) wholemeal (whole-wheat) flour
50g/2oz/½ cup plain (all-purpose) white flour
5ml/1 tsp baking powder
2.5ml/½ tsp ground cinnamon
60ml/4 tbsp skimmed milk
2.5ml/½ tsp vanilla essence (extract)
10ml/2 tsp icing (confectioners') sugar
low-fat ready-to-serve custard, to serve

Cook's Tip

For a simple sauce, blend 5ml/1 tsp arrowroot with 15ml/1 tbsp peach juice in a small pan. Stir in the remaining peach juice from the can and bring to the boil. Simmer for 1 minute until thickened and clear.

Nutritional information

Calories	255kcal/1071kj
Fat	6.8g
Saturated fat	0.9g
Cholesterol	35mg
Fibre	2.7g

2 Put all the remaining ingredients, except the icing sugar, into a mixing bowl. Beat for 3–4 minutes, until mixed.

3 Spoon the sponge mixture over the peaches and level the top evenly. Cook in the oven for 35–40 minutes, or until springy to the touch.

CAKES

You can indulge in these cakes without worrying about fat, cholesterol or your waistline. Although they are all made with alternative low-fat ingredients, there is no compromise on flavour, and they all taste delicious.

Coffee Sponge Drops

These are scrumptious on their own, but taste even better with a filling made by mixing low-fat soft cheese with drained and chopped stem ginger.

MAKES 12

50g/2oz/½ cup plain
   (all-purpose) flour
15ml/1 tbsp instant coffee powder
2 eggs
75g/3oz/6 tbsp caster
   (superfine) sugar

For the filling

115g/4oz/½ cup low-fat
   soft (farmer's) cheese
40g/1½oz/¼ cup chopped
   preserved stem ginger

1 Preheat the oven to 190°C/375°F/ Gas 5. Line two baking sheets with baking parchment. Make the filling by beating together the soft cheese and stem ginger. Chill until required. Sift the flour and instant coffee powder together.

3 Carefully add the sifted flour and coffee mixture and gently fold in with a metal spoon, being careful not to knock out any air.

2 Combine the eggs and caster sugar in a bowl. Beat with a hand-held electric whisk until thick and mousse-like. (When the whisk is lifted, a trail should remain on the surface of the mixture for at least 15 seconds.)

4 Spoon the mixture into a piping (pastry) bag fitted with a 1cm/½in plain nozzle. Pipe 4cm/1½in rounds on the baking sheets. Bake for 12 minutes. Cool on a wire rack, then sandwich together with the filling.

5 Bake for 12 minutes. Cool on a wire rack, then sandwich together with the filling.

Variation

For the filling, try chopped walnuts or pecan nuts as an alternative to stem ginger. Or, add 5ml/1 tsp vanilla extract to the low-fat cheese for the filling.

Nutritional information	
Calories	69kcal/290kj
Fat	1.36g
Saturated fat	0.5g
Cholesterol	33mg
Fibre	0.3g

Ginger Cake with Spiced Cream

A spicy and comforting cake, ideal for winter evenings.

SERVES 9

175g/6oz/1½ cups plain
  (all-purpose) flour
10ml/2 tsp baking powder
2.5ml/½ tsp salt
10ml/2 tsp ground ginger
10ml/2 tsp ground cinnamon
5ml/1 tsp ground cloves
1.5ml/¼ tsp freshly ground nutmeg
2 eggs
200g/7oz/1 cup granulated sugar
250ml/8fl oz/1 cup whipping cream
5ml/1 tsp vanilla essence (extract)
icing (confectioners') sugar, to decorate

For the spiced whipped cream

175ml/6fl oz/¾ cup low-fat
  whipping cream
5ml/1 tsp icing (confectioners') sugar
1.5ml/¼ tsp ground cinnamon
1.5ml/¼ tsp ground ginger
0.75ml/⅛ tsp freshly grated nutmeg

1 Preheat the oven to 180°C/350°F/
Gas 4. Grease a 23cm/9in square
baking tin (pan).

2 Sift the flour, baking powder, salt,
ginger, cinnamon, cloves and nutmeg
into a bowl. Set aside.

3 With an electric mixer, beat the eggs
on a high speed until very thick, for
about 5 minutes. Gradually beat in the
granulated sugar.

4 With the mixer on a low speed, beat
in the flour mixture alternately with
the cream into the eggs, beginning and
ending with the flour. Stir in the vanilla.

5 Pour into the tin and bake for
35–40 minutes, until the top springs
back when touched lightly. Leave to cool
in the tin on a wire rack for 10 minutes.

6 For the spiced cream, mix the
ingredients and whip until the cream
holds soft peaks. Sprinkle the hot cake
with icing sugar and serve with the cream.

Nutritional information	
Calories	305kcal/1282kj
Fat	11.6g
Saturated fat	6.6g
Cholesterol	69mg
Fibre	0.8g

Spiced Apple Cake

Grated apple and chopped dates give this cake a natural sweetness.

SERVES 8

225g/8oz/2 cups self-raising (self-rising)
    wholemeal (whole-wheat) flour

5ml/1 tsp baking powder

10ml/2 tsp ground cinnamon

175g/6oz/1 cup chopped dates

2 eating apples

75g/3oz/scant ½ cup light muscovado
    (light brown) sugar

15ml/1 tbsp pear and apple spread

120ml/4fl oz/½ cup apple juice

2 eggs

90ml/6 tbsp sunflower oil

15ml/1 tbsp chopped walnuts

1 Preheat the oven to 180°C/350°F/
Gas 4. Grease and line a deep round
20cm/8in cake tin (pan). Sift the flour,
baking powder and cinnamon into a
mixing bowl, then mix in the dates and
make a well in the centre. Core and grate
the apples.

Variation

Omit 25g/1oz/2 tbsp sugar if the fruit is
very sweet. It is not necessary to peel the
apples – the skin adds extra fibre and
softens on cooking.

Nutritional information

Calories	331kcal/1389kj
Fat	11.4g
Saturated fat	1.7g
Cholesterol	48mg
Fibre	2.5g

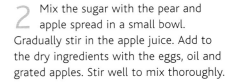

2 Mix the sugar with the pear and
apple spread in a small bowl.
Gradually stir in the apple juice. Add to
the dry ingredients with the eggs, oil and
grated apples. Stir well to mix thoroughly.

3 Spoon the mixture into the prepared
cake tin, sprinkle liberally with the
walnuts and bake for 60–65 minutes or
until a skewer inserted into the centre of
the cake comes out clean. Transfer to a
wire rack, remove the lining paper and
leave to cool.

Banana and Gingerbread Slices

This cake is very quick to make and deliciously moist due to the addition of bananas.

SERVES 20

275g/10oz/2½ cups plain
   (all-purpose) flour
20ml/4 tsp ground ginger
10ml/2 tsp mixed (apple pie) spice
5ml/1 tsp bicarbonate of soda
   (baking soda)
115g/4oz/½ cup soft light
   brown sugar
60ml/4 tbsp sunflower oil
30ml/2 tbsp molasses or
   black treacle
30ml/2 tbsp malt extract
2 eggs
60ml/4 tbsp orange juice
3 ripe bananas
115g/4oz/scant 1 cup raisins

Variation

To make Spiced Honey and Banana Cake; omit the ground ginger and add another 5ml/1 tsp mixed spice; omit the malt extract and the molasses or treacle and add 60ml/4 tbsp strong-flavoured clear honey instead; and replace the raisins with either sultanas (golden raisins), coarsely chopped ready-to-eat dried apricots or semi-dried pineapple. If you choose to use the pineapple, then you could also replace the orange juice with fresh pineapple juice.

Cook's Tip

The flavour of this cake develops as it keeps, so if you can, store it for a few days before eating.

Nutritional information

Calories	148kcal/621kj
Fat	3.1g
Saturated fat	0.5g
Cholesterol	19.3mg
Fibre	0.8g

1 Preheat the oven to 180°C/350°F/ Gas 4. Lightly grease and line an 18 x 28cm/7 x 11in baking tin (pan).

2 Sift the flour into a bowl with the spices and bicarbonate of soda. Mix in the sugar with some of the flour and sift it all into the bowl.

3 Make a well in the centre, add the oil, molasses or black treacle, malt extract, eggs and orange juice and mix together thoroughly.

4 Mash the bananas, then add them to the bowl with the raisins. Use a wooden spoon and combine the mixture thoroughly.

5 Pour the mixture into the prepared baking tin and bake for about 35–40 minutes, or until the centre springs back when lightly pressed.

6 Leave the cake in the tin to cool for 5 minutes, then turn out on to a wire rack and leave to cool completely. Cut into 20 slices.

Eggless Christmas Cake

This is an inventive way to create a low-calorie Christmas treat.

SERVES 12

75g/3oz/¹⁄₃ cup glacé
   (candied) cherries
75g/3oz/¹⁄₂ cup sultanas
   (golden raisins)
75g/3oz/generous ¹⁄₂ cup raisins
75g/3oz/¹⁄₃ cup currants
50g/2oz/¹⁄₃ cup cut mixed peel
250ml/8fl oz/1 cup apple juice
25g/1oz/2 tbsp toasted hazelnuts
30ml/2 tbsp pumpkin seeds
2 pieces preserved stem ginger in
   syrup, chopped
finely grated rind of 1 lemon
120ml/4fl oz/¹⁄₂ cup
   skimmed milk
120ml/4fl oz/¹⁄₂ cup sunflower oil
225g/8oz/2 cups wholemeal (whole-
   wheat) self-raising (self-rising) flour
10ml/2 tsp mixed (apple pie) spice
45ml/3 tbsp brandy or dark rum
apricot jam, for brushing
glacé (candied) fruits, to decorate

1 Halve the cherries and place them with the sultanas, raisins, currants and mixed peel in a bowl. Stir in the apple juice, cover and leave the fruit to soak overnight.

2 Preheat the oven to 150°C/300°F/ Gas 2.

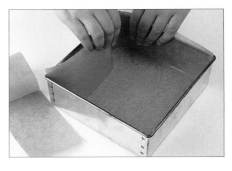

3 Lightly grease and line an 18cm/7in square cake tin (pan).

4 Add the hazelnuts, pumpkin seeds, ginger and lemon rind to the soaked fruit. Stir in the milk and oil. Sift the flour and spice. Stir in with the brandy or rum.

5 Spoon into the tin and bake for 30 minutes. Cool on a wire rack. Brush with jam and decorate with fruits.

Nutritional information

Calories	225kcal/946kj
Fat	6.1g
Saturated fat	0.9g
Cholesterol	0.2mg
Fibre	2.5g

Angel Cake

A delightfully light cake to serve as a dessert for a special occasion.

1 Preheat the oven to 180°C/350°F/ Gas 4. Sift both flours on to a sheet of baking parchment.

2 Whisk the egg whites in a large clean, dry bowl until very stiff, then gradually add the sugar and vanilla essence, whisking until the mixture is thick and glossy.

3 Gently fold in the flour mixture with a large metal spoon. Spoon into an ungreased 25cm/10in angel cake tin (pan), smooth the surface and bake for about 45–50 minutes, until the cake springs back when lightly pressed.

4 Sprinkle a piece of baking parchment with caster sugar and set an egg cup in the centre. Invert the cake tin over the paper, balancing it carefully on the egg cup. When cold, the cake will drop out of the tin. Transfer it to a plate, spoon over the glacé icing, arrange the physalis on top then dust with icing sugar and serve.

SERVES 10

40g/1½oz/⅓ cup cornflour (cornstarch)
40g/1½oz/⅓ cup plain (all-purpose) flour
8 egg whites
225g/8oz/generous 1 cup caster (superfine) sugar, plus extra for sprinkling
5ml/1 tsp vanilla essence (extract)
90ml/6 tbsp orange-flavoured glacé icing, 4–6 physalis and a little icing (confectioners') sugar, to decorate

Nutritional information	
Calories	139kcal/582kj
Fat	0.1g
Saturated fat	0.1g
Cholesterol	0mg
Fibre	0.1g

Peach Roll

A feather-light sponge enclosing peach jam is just what is required at tea time.

SERVES 6–8

3 eggs

115g/4oz/generous ½ cup caster (superfine) sugar, plus extra for sprinkling

75g/3oz/⅔ cup plain (all-purpose) flour, sifted

15ml/1 tbsp boiling water

90ml/6 tbsp peach jam

glacé icing (see Cook's Tip) or icing (confectioners') sugar, for dusting (optional)

Cook's Tip

To decorate the Swiss roll with glacé icing, make the icing with 115g/4oz/1 cup icing sugar and enough warm water to make a thin glacé icing. Put in a piping (pastry) bag fitted with a small writing nozzle and pipe lines over the top.

Nutritional information

Calories	178kcal/746kj
Fat	2.5g
Saturated fat	0.7g
Cholesterol	82.5mg
Fibre	0.3g

1 Preheat the oven to 200°C/400°F/ Gas 6. Grease a 30 x 20cm/12 x 8in Swiss roll tin (jelly roll pan) and line with baking parchment. Combine the eggs and sugar in a bowl. Beat with a hand-held electric whisk until thick and mousse-like. (When the whisk is lifted, a trail should remain on the surface of the mixture for at least 15 seconds.)

2 Carefully fold in the flour with a large metal spoon, then add the boiling water in the same way.

3 Spoon into the tin and bake for about 10–12 minutes until the cake springs back when lightly pressed.

4 Spread a sheet of baking parchment on a flat surface, sprinkle it with caster sugar, then invert the cake on top. Peel off the lining paper.

5 Neatly trim the edges of the cake. Make a neat cut two-thirds of the way through the cake, about 1cm/½in from the short edge nearest you.

6 Spread the cake with the peach jam and roll up quickly from the partially cut end. Hold in position for a minute, making sure the join is underneath. Cool the cake on a wire rack. Decorate with glacé icing or dust with icing sugar before serving.

Nectarine Amaretto Cake

Amaretto liqueur adds a hint of luxury to this fruity cake.

1 Preheat the oven to 180°C/350°F/ Gas 4. Grease a 20cm/8in round, loose-bottomed cake tin (pan). Whisk together the egg yolks, caster sugar, lemon rind and juice in a bowl until the mixture is thick, pale and creamy.

2 Fold in the semolina, almonds and flour until smooth.

3 Whisk the egg whites in a bowl until fairly stiff. Use a metal spoon to stir a generous spoonful of the whites into the semolina mixture, then fold in the remaining egg whites. Spoon the mixture into the cake tin.

4 Bake for 30–35 minutes until the centre of the cake springs back when pressed lightly. Remove from the oven and loosen around the edge with a metal spatula. Prick the top with a skewer. Leave to cool in the tin.

5 To make the syrup, heat the sugar and water in a small pan, stirring until the sugar is dissolved. Boil without stirring for 2 minutes. Add the amaretto liqueur and drizzle the liqueur syrup over the cake in the tin.

6 Remove the cake from the tin and transfer to a serving plate. Slice the nectarines and arrange them on top of the cake. Brush with warm apricot glaze.

SERVES 8

3 eggs, separated
175g/6oz/¾ cup caster (superfine) sugar
grated rind and juice of 1 lemon
50g/2oz/⅓ cup semolina
25g/1oz/¼ cup ground almonds
25g/1oz/¼ cup plain (all-purpose) flour
2 nectarines, halved and stoned (pitted)
60ml/4 tbsp apricot glaze

For the syrup

45g/3oz/⅓ cup caster (superfine) sugar
90ml/6 tbsp water
30ml/2 tbsp amaretto liqueur

Nutritional information	
Calories	264kcal/1108kj
Fat	5.7g
Saturated fat	0.9g
Cholesterol	72mg
Fibre	1.1g

Apple and Pear Skillet Cake

An unusual, spicy cake, prepared on the hob and then baked in the oven.

1 Preheat the oven to 190°C/375°F/ Gas 5. In a mixing bowl, toss together the apple slices, pear slices, walnuts, cinnamon and nutmeg. Set aside.

2 With an electric mixer, beat together the eggs, flour, brown sugar, milk and vanilla.

3 Melt the butter or margarine in a 23cm/9in ovenproof skillet over a medium heat. Add the apple mixture. Cook until lightly caramelized, for about 5 minutes, stirring occasionally.

4 Pour the batter over the fruit and nuts. Transfer the skillet to the oven and bake for about 30 minutes, until the cake is puffy and pulling away from the sides of the pan.

5 Sprinkle the cake lightly with icing sugar and serve hot.

SERVES 6

1 apple, peeled, cored and thinly sliced
1 pear, peeled, cored and thinly sliced
50g/2oz/½ cup walnut
   pieces, chopped
5ml/1 tsp ground cinnamon
5ml/1 tsp freshly grated nutmeg
3 eggs
75g/3oz/⅔ cup plain
   (all-purpose) flour
30ml/2 tbsp light brown sugar
175ml/6fl oz/¾ cup skimmed milk
5ml/1 tsp vanilla essence (extract)
60ml/4 tbsp butter or margarine
icing (confectioners') sugar, for sprinkling

Nutritional information	
Calories	315kcal/1311kj
Fat	19.9g
Saturated fat	3.3g
Cholesterol	98mg
Fibre	1.8g

Chocolate and Orange Angel Cake

This light-as-air sponge with its fluffy icing is virtually fat free, yet tastes heavenly.

SERVES 10

25g/1oz/¼ cup plain
   (all-purpose) flour
15g/½oz/2 tbsp reduced-fat cocoa
   powder (unsweetened)
15g/½oz/2 tbsp cornflour (cornstarch)
pinch of salt
5 egg whites
2.5ml/½ tsp cream of tartar
   (tartaric acid)
115g/4oz/scant ½ cup caster
   (superfine) sugar
blanched and shredded rind of
   1 orange, to decorate

For the icing

200g/7oz/scant 1 cup caster
   (superfine) sugar
1 egg white

Nutritional information

Calories	153kcal/644kj
Fat	0.3g
Saturated fat	0.1g
Cholesterol	0mg
Fibre	0.3g

1 Preheat the oven to 180°C/350°F/ Gas 4. Sift the flour, cocoa powder, cornflour and salt together three times. Beat the egg whites in a large clean, dry bowl until foamy. Add the cream of tartar, then whisk until soft peaks form.

2 Add the caster sugar to the egg whites a spoonful at a time, whisking after each addition. Sift a third of the flour and cocoa mixture over the meringue and gently fold in. Repeat, sifting and folding in the flour and cocoa mixture two more times.

3 Spoon the mixture into a non-stick 20cm/8in ring mould and level the top. Bake for 35 minutes. Turn upside down on to a wire rack and cool in the tin (pan). Carefully ease out of the tin.

4 For the icing, put the sugar in a pan with 75ml/5 tbsp cold water. Stir over a low heat until dissolved. Boil until the syrup reaches a temperature of 119°C/ 238°F on a sugar thermometer or when a drop of the syrup makes a soft ball when dripped into a cup of cold water. Remove from the heat.

5 Whisk the egg white until stiff. Add the syrup in a thin stream, whisking all the time. Continue to whisk until the mixture is very thick and fluffy.

6 Spread the icing over the top and sides of the cooled cake. Sprinkle the orange rind over the top of the cake and serve.

Chocolate Banana Cake

A chocolate cake that's deliciously low in fat — it is moist enough to eat without the icing if you want to cut down on calories.

SERVES 8

225g/8oz/2 cups self-raising (self-rising) flour
45ml/3 tbsp reduced-fat cocoa powder (unsweetened)
115g/4oz/½ cup light muscovado (brown) sugar
30ml/2 tbsp malt extract
30ml/2 tbsp golden (light corn) syrup
2 eggs
60ml/4 tbsp skimmed milk
60ml/4 tbsp sunflower oil
2 large ripe bananas

For the icing

225g/8oz/2 cups icing (confectioners') sugar, sifted
35ml/7 tsp reduced-fat cocoa powder, sifted
15–30ml/1–2 tbsp warm water

Cook's Tip

To add a contrasting decoration, make a thinner, lighter icing by mixing the remaining icing sugar and cocoa powder with a few drops of water. Drizzle or pipe this icing across the top of the cake to decorate.

Nutritional information

Calories	411kcal/1727kj
Fat	9g
Saturated fat	2.1g
Cholesterol	48mg
Fibre	2.1g

1 Preheat the oven to 160°C/325°F/ Gas 3. Grease and line a deep round 20cm/8in cake tin (pan).

2 Sift the flour into a mixing bowl with the cocoa powder. Stir in the sugar.

3 Make a well in the centre and add the malt extract, golden syrup, eggs, milk and oil. Mash the bananas thoroughly and stir them into the mixture until completely combined.

4 Pour the cake mixture into the tin and bake for 1–1¼ hours or until the centre of the cake springs back when lightly pressed.

5 Remove the cake from the tin and leave on a wire rack to cool.

6 Reserve 50g/2oz/⅓ cup icing sugar and 5ml/1 tsp cocoa powder. Make a dark icing by beating the remaining sugar and cocoa powder with enough of the warm water to make a thick icing. Pour it over the top of the cake and spread evenly to the edges.

Tia Maria Gâteau

This feather-light coffee sponge has a creamy liqueur-flavoured filling.

SERVES 8

75g/3oz/²⁄₃ cup plain
    (all-purpose) flour
30ml/2 tbsp instant coffee powder
3 eggs
115g/4oz/generous ½ cup caster
    (superfine) sugar
coffee beans, to decorate (optional)

For the filling

175g/6oz/¾ cup low-fat
    soft cheese
15ml/1 tbsp clear honey
15ml/1 tbsp Tia Maria liqueur
50g/2oz/¼ cup preserved stem ginger,
    roughly chopped

For the icing

225g/8oz/2 cups icing
    (confectioners') sugar, sifted
10ml/2 tsp coffee essence
15ml/1 tbsp water
5ml/1 tsp reduced-fat cocoa
    powder (unsweetened)

Cook's Tip

When folding in the flour mixture in step 3, be careful not to remove the air, as it helps the cake to rise.

Nutritional information

Calories	226kcal/951kj
Fat	3.1g
Saturated fat	1.2g
Cholesterol	75mg
Fibre	0.6g

1 Preheat the oven to 190°C/375°F/ Gas 5. Grease and line a 20cm/8in deep round cake tin (pan). Sift the flour and coffee powder together on to a sheet of baking parchment.

2 Whisk the eggs and sugar in a bowl until thick and mousse-like. (When the whisk is lifted, a trail should remain on the surface of the mixture for at least 15 seconds.)

3 Fold in the flour mixture. Turn the mixture into the prepared tin. Bake the sponge for 30–35 minutes or until it springs back when lightly pressed. Turn on to a wire rack to cool completely.

4 To make the filling, mix the soft cheese with the honey in a bowl. Beat until smooth, then stir in the Tia Maria and chopped stem ginger.

5 Split the cake in half horizontally and sandwich the two halves together with the Tia Maria filling.

6 Make the icing. In a bowl, mix the icing sugar and coffee essence with enough of the water to make a consistency that will coat the back of a wooden spoon. Pour three-quarters of the icing over the cake, spreading it evenly to the edges.

7 Stir the cocoa into the remaining icing over the cake. Spoon into a piping (pastry) bag fitted with a writing nozzle and pipe the mocha icing over the coffee icing. Decorate with coffee beans, if liked.

COOKIES, BARS AND BUNS

Served straight from the oven, these bitesize bakes are sure to become family favourites, and you can enjoy them too, because they are low in fat and cholesterol.

Banana and Apricot Chelsea Buns

These buns are old favourites given a low-fat twist with a delectable fruit filling.

SERVES 9

about 90ml/6 tbsp warm
   skimmed milk
5ml/1 tsp active dried yeast
pinch of sugar
225g/8oz/2 cups strong white
   bread flour
10ml/2 tsp mixed (apple pie) spice
2.5ml/½ tsp salt
50g/2oz/¼ cup caster
   (superfine) sugar
25g/1oz/2 tbsp soft margarine
1 egg

For the filling

1 large ripe banana
175g/6oz/1 cup ready-to-eat
   dried apricots
30ml/2 tbsp caster (superfine) sugar
30ml/2 tbsp light muscovado
   (brown) sugar

For the glaze

30ml/2 tbsp caster
   (superfine) sugar
30ml/2 tbsp water

Cook's Tip

Do not leave the buns in the tin for too
long or the glaze will stick to the sides,
making them very difficult to remove.

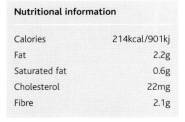

Nutritional information

Calories	214kcal/901kj
Fat	2.2g
Saturated fat	0.6g
Cholesterol	22mg
Fibre	2.1g

1 Lightly grease an 18cm/7in square tin. Put the warm milk in a jug and sprinkle the yeast on top. Add a pinch of sugar to help activate the yeast, mix well and leave for 30 minutes.

2 Sift the flour, spice and salt into a mixing bowl. Stir in the caster sugar, rub in the margarine, then stir in the yeast mixture and the egg. Gradually mix in the flour to make a soft dough, adding extra milk if needed.

3 Turn out the dough on to a floured surface and knead for 5 minutes until smooth and elastic. Return the dough to the clean bowl, cover with a damp tea towel and leave in a warm place for about 2 hours, until doubled in bulk.

4 To prepare the filling, mash the banana in a bowl. Using scissors, snip the apricots into pieces, then stir into the banana with the sugars.

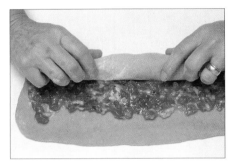

5 Knead the dough on a floured surface for 2 minutes, then roll out to a 30 x 23cm/12 x 9in rectangle. Spread the banana and apricot filling over the dough and roll up lengthways like a Swiss (jelly) roll, with the join underneath.

6 Cut the roll into nine buns. Place, cut side down, in the tin, cover and leave to rise for 30 minutes. Preheat the oven to 200°C/400°F/Gas 6 and bake for 20–25 minutes. Mix the caster sugar and water in a small pan. Heat, stirring, until dissolved, then boil for 2 minutes. Brush the glaze over the buns while still hot.

Prune and Peel Rock Buns

Split these buns and serve with fromage frais or ricotta cheese, if you like.

MAKES 12

225g/8oz/2 cups plain (all-purpose) flour
10ml/2 tsp baking powder
75g/3oz/⅓ cup demerara (raw) sugar
50g/2oz/¼ cup chopped ready-to-eat dried prunes
50g/2oz/⅓ cup chopped mixed peel
finely grated rind of 1 lemon
50ml/2fl oz/¼ cup sunflower oil
75ml/5 tbsp skimmed milk

1 Preheat the oven to 200°C/400°F/ Gas 6. Lightly oil a large baking sheet. Sift together the flour and baking powder, then stir in the sugar, prunes, peel and lemon rind.

2 Mix the oil and milk, then stir into the mixture, to make a dough that just binds together.

3 Spoon into rocky heaps on the baking sheet and bake for 20 minutes, until golden. Cool the buns on a wire rack.

Nutritional information

Calories	135kcal/570kj
Fat	3.4g
Saturated fat	0.4g
Cholesterol	0.1mg
Fibre	0.9g

Chewy Fruit Muesli Slice

Although these are low in fat and high in fibre, they taste delicious.

MAKES 8 SLICES

75g/3oz/scant ½ cup ready-to-eat
    dried apricots, chopped
1 eating apple, cored and grated
150g/5oz/1¼ cups
    Swiss-style muesli
150ml/¼ pint/⅔ cup apple juice
15g/½oz/1 tbsp soft
    sunflower margarine

1 Preheat the oven to 190°C/375°F/
Gas 5. Place all the ingredients in
a large bowl and mix well. Press the
mixture into a 20cm/8in round, non-stick
sandwich tin (pan) and bake for 35–40
minutes, or until lightly browned and firm.

2 Mark the muesli slice into eight
wedges and leave to cool in the tin.

Nutritional information	
Calories	112kcal/467kj
Fat	2.8g
Saturated fat	0.5g
Cholesterol	0.1mg
Fibre	2.1g

Blueberry Streusel Slice
The soft berry filling makes a good contrast to the nutty topping.

MAKES ABOUT 30 SLICES

225g/8oz shortcrust (unsweetened) pastry, thawed if frozen
50g/2oz/½ cup plain (all-purpose) flour
1.5ml/¼ tsp baking powder
40g/1½oz/3 tbsp butter or margarine
50g/2oz/¼ cup soft light brown sugar
25g/1oz/½ cup fresh white breadcrumbs
1.5ml/¼ tsp salt
50g/2oz/½ cup flaked (sliced) almonds
30ml/4 tbsp blackberry or bramble jelly
115g/4oz/1 cup blueberries

Nutritional information

Calories	77kcal/322kj
Fat	4.2g
Saturated fat	1.6g
Cholesterol	5.8mg
Fibre	1g

1 Preheat the oven to 180°F/350°F/ Gas 4. Roll out the pastry on a lightly floured surface to line an 18 x 28cm/ 7 x 11in Swiss roll tin (jelly roll pan). Prick the base evenly with a fork.

2 Rub together the flour, baking powder, butter or margarine, sugar, breadcrumbs and salt until crumbly, then mix in the almonds.

3 Spread the pastry with the jelly, sprinkle with the blueberries, then cover evenly with the almond mixture, pressing down lightly. Bake for 20 minutes, then reduce the temperature to 160°C/ 325°F/Gas 3 and cook for a further 10–20 minutes.

4 Remove from the oven when golden on the top and the pastry is cooked through. Cut into slices while still hot, then allow to cool.

COOKIES, BARS AND BUNS 75

Sticky Date and Apple Bars

If possible, allow this mixture to mature for 1–2 days before cutting – it will get stickier and better!

MAKES ABOUT 16 BARS

115g/4oz/1/2 cup margarine
50g/2oz/1/4 cup soft dark brown sugar
50g/2oz/4 tbsp golden (light corn) syrup
115g/4oz/3/4 cup chopped dates
115g/4oz/generous 1 cup rolled oats
115g/4oz/1 cup self-raising (self-rising)
    wholemeal (whole-wheat) flour
225g/8oz eating apples, peeled, cored
    and grated, and sprinkled with
    5–10ml/1–2 tsp lemon juice
20–25 walnut halves

1 Preheat the oven to 190°C/375°F/ Gas 5. Line an 18–20cm/7–8in square or rectangular loose-based cake tin (pan). In a large pan, heat the margarine, sugar, syrup and dates, stirring until the dates soften completely.

2 Gradually work in the oats, flour and apples until well mixed. Spoon into the tin and spread out evenly. Top with the walnut halves.

3 Bake for 30 minutes, then reduce the temperature to 160°C/325°F/Gas 3 and bake for 10–20 minutes more, until firm to the touch. Cut into squares or bars while still warm. Keep for 1–2 days.

Nutritional information	
Calories	183kcal/763kj
Fat	10.1g
Saturated fat	1.6g
Cholesterol	0.1mg
Fibre	1g

Apricot Sponge Bars

These delectable fingers are perfect for tea time – the apricots keep them moist for several days.

MAKES 18

225g/8oz/2 cups self-raising
    (self-rising) flour
115g/4oz/½ cup soft light
    brown sugar
50g/2oz/⅓ cup semolina
175g/6oz/¾ cup ready-to-eat dried
    apricots, chopped
30ml/2 tbsp clear honey
30ml/2 tbsp malt extract
2 eggs
60ml/4 tbsp skimmed milk
60ml/4 tbsp sunflower oil
a few drops of almond essence (extract)
30ml/2 tbsp flaked (sliced) almonds

Nutritional information

Calories	153kcal/641kj
Fat	4.5g
Saturated fat	0.6g
Cholesterol	21.5mg
Fibre	1.3g

1 Preheat the oven to 160°C/325°F/ Gas 3. Lightly grease and then line an 18 x 28cm/7 x 11in baking tin (pan).

2 Sift the flour into a bowl and mix in the sugar, semolina and apricots. Make a well in the centre and add the honey, malt extract, eggs, milk, oil and almond essence. Mix the ingredients together thoroughly until smooth.

3 Spoon the mixture into the tin, spreading it to the edges, then sprinkle over the flaked almonds.

4 Bake for 30–35 minutes, or until the centre springs back when lightly pressed. Remove from the tin and turn on to a wire rack to cool. Cut into 18 slices using a sharp knife.

Cook's Tip

If you can't find pre-soaked apricots, use chopped ordinary dried apricots soaked in boiling water for 1 hour, then drain and add to the mixture.

Apricot Yogurt Cookies

These soft cookies are very quick to make and are useful for lunch boxes.

1 Preheat the oven to 190°C/375°F/ Gas 5. Lightly oil a large baking sheet.

2 Sift together the flour, baking powder and cinnamon. Stir in the oats, sugar, apricots and nuts.

3 Beat together the yogurt and oil, then stir the mixture evenly into the mixture to make a firm dough. If necessary, add a little more yogurt.

4 Use your hands to roll the mixture into about 16 small balls, place on the baking sheet and flatten with a fork.

5 Sprinkle with demerara sugar. Bake the cookies for 15–20 minutes, or until firm and golden brown. Leave to cool on a wire rack.

MAKES 16

175g/6oz/1½ cups plain
  (all-purpose) flour
5ml/1 tsp baking powder
5ml/1 tsp ground cinnamon
75g/3oz/scant 1 cup rolled oats
75g/3oz/⅓ cup light muscovado
  (light brown) sugar
115g/4oz/½ cup chopped ready-to-eat
  dried apricots
15ml/1 tbsp flaked (sliced) hazelnuts
  or almonds
50g/5oz/⅔ cup natural (plain) yogurt
45ml/3 tbsp sunflower oil
demerara (raw) sugar, to sprinkle

Cook's Tip

These cookies do not keep well, so it is best to eat them within two days, or to freeze them. Pack into polythene bags and freeze for up to four months.

Nutritional information

Calories	95kcal/400kj
Fat	2.7g
Saturated fat	0.4g
Cholesterol	0.3mg
Fibre	0.9g

Oaty Crisps

These cookies are very crisp and crunchy – ideal to serve with a cup of tea.

MAKES 18

175g/6oz/1½ cups rolled oats
75g/3oz/⅓ cup light muscovado
   (light brown) sugar
1 egg
60ml/4 tbsp sunflower oil
30ml/2 tbsp malt extract

Nutritional information

Calories	86kcal/360kj
Fat	3.6g
Saturated fat	0.6g
Cholesterol	10.7mg
Fibre	0.7g

1 Preheat the oven to 190°C/375°F/ Gas 5. Grease two baking sheets. Mix the oats and sugar in a bowl, and break up any lumps in the sugar. Add the egg, sunflower oil and malt extract, mix well, then leave to soak for 15 minutes.

2 Using a teaspoon, place small mounds of the mixture well apart on the prepared baking sheets. Press the mounds into 7.5cm/3in rounds with the back of a dampened fork.

3 Bake the cookies for 10–15 minutes until golden brown. Leave them to cool for 1 minute, then remove with a palette knife (metal spatula) and cool on a wire rack.

Cook's Tip

To give these biscuits a coarser texture, substitute jumbo oats for some or all of the rolled oats. Once cool, store the biscuits in an airtight container to keep them as crisp and fresh as possible.

Orange Cookies

These tangy cookies are a popular choice for a well-earned coffee break.

1 With an electric mixer, cream the butter and sugar until light and fluffy. Add the yolks, orange juice and rind, and continue beating to blend. Set aside.

2 In another bowl, sift together the flours, salt and baking powder. Add to the butter mixture and stir until it forms a dough.

3 Wrap the dough in baking parchment and chill for 2 hours.

4 Preheat the oven to 190°C/375°F/ Gas 5. Grease two baking sheets.

5 Roll spoonfuls of the dough into balls and place 2.5–5cm/1–2in apart on the prepared sheets.

6 Press down with a fork to flatten. Bake for 8–10 minutes, until golden brown. With a metal spatula, transfer to a rack to cool.

MAKES 30

115g/4oz/½ cup butter
200g/7oz/1 cup caster (superfine) sugar
2 egg yolks
15ml/1 tbsp fresh orange juice
grated rind of 1 orange
175g/6oz/1½ cups plain
   (all-purpose) flour
115g/4oz/½ cup self-raising
   (self-rising) flour
2.5ml/½ tsp salt
5ml/1 tsp baking powder

Nutritional information	
Calories	84kcal/353kj
Fat	3.5g
Saturated fat	0.7g
Cholesterol	14mg
Fibre	0.2g

TEA BREADS

These light and tasty tea breads are sweetened with honey and fruits, and enhanced with warm spices such as ginger, cinnamon and nutmeg. They make a perfect mid-afternoon energy booster when served with a cup of tea or coffee.

Banana and Cardamom Bread

The combination of banana and cardamom is delicious in this soft-textured moist loaf.
It is perfect for tea time, served with low-fat spread and jam.

MAKES 1 LOAF

150ml/¼ pint/⅔ cup lukewarm water
5ml/1 tsp active dried yeast
pinch of sugar
10 cardamom pods
400g/14oz/3½ cups strong white
    bread flour
5ml/1 tsp salt
30ml/2 tbsp malt extract
2 ripe bananas, mashed
5ml/1 tsp sesame seeds

Cook's Tip

Make sure that the bananas are really
ripe, so that they impart maximum
flavour to the bread. If you prefer,
place the dough in one piece in a
450g/1lb loaf tin (pan) and bake for
an extra 5 minutes. As well as being
low in fat, bananas are a good source
of potassium, therefore making an
ideal nutritious, low-fat snack.

1 Put the warm water in a small bowl.
Sprinkle the yeast on top. Add the
sugar, mix well and leave for 10 minutes.

2 Split the cardamom pods. Remove
the seeds and chop them finely.

3 Sift the flour and salt into a mixing
bowl and make a well in the centre.
Add the yeast mixture with the malt
extract, chopped cardamom seeds
and bananas.

4 Gradually incorporate the flour and
mix to a soft dough, adding a little
extra water if necessary. Turn the dough
on to a floured surface and knead for
about 5 minutes until smooth and elastic.
Return to the clean bowl, cover with a
damp dishtowel and leave to rise for
about 2 hours, until doubled in bulk.

5 Grease a baking sheet. Turn the
dough on to a floured surface, knead
briefly, then divide into three and shape
into a braid. Place the braid on the baking
sheet and cover loosely with a large
plastic bag (ballooning it to trap the air).
Leave until well risen. Preheat the oven
to 220°C/425°F/Gas 7.

6 Brush the braid lightly with water
and sprinkle with the sesame seeds.
Bake for 10 minutes, then lower the oven
temperature to 200°C/400°F/Gas 6.
Cook for 15 minutes more, or until the
loaf sounds hollow when it is tapped
underneath. Cool on a wire rack.

Nutritional information	
Calories	299kcal/1254kj
Fat	1.6g
Saturated fat	0.2g
Cholesterol	0mg
Fibre	2.7g

Banana Orange Loaf

For the best banana flavour and a really good, moist texture, make sure the bananas are very ripe for this cake.

MAKES 1 LOAF

90g/3½oz/¾ cup plain (all-purpose) wholemeal (whole-wheat) flour

90g/3½oz/¾ cup plain (all-purpose) flour

5ml/1 tsp baking powder

5ml/1 tsp mixed (apple pie) spice

45ml/3 tbsp flaked (sliced) hazelnuts, toasted

2 large ripe bananas

1 egg

30ml/2 tbsp sunflower oil

30ml/2 tbsp clear honey

finely grated rind and juice of 1 small orange

4 orange slices, halved

10ml/2 tsp icing (confectioners') sugar

Nutritional information

Calories	217kcal/911kj
Fat	7.6g
Saturated fat	0.9g
Cholesterol	24mg
Fibre	2.5g

1 Preheat the oven to 180°C/350°F/ Gas 4.

2 Brush a 1 litre/1¾ pint/4 cup loaf tin (pan) with sunflower oil and line the base with baking parchment.

3 Sift the wholemeal flour and plain flour with the baking powder and spice into a large bowl, adding any bran caught in the sieve. Stir the toasted hazelnuts into the dry ingredients.

4 Peel and mash the bananas. Beat with the egg, oil, honey, orange rind and juice. Stir into the dry ingredients.

5 Spoon the mixture into the prepared tin and smooth the top. Bake for 40–45 minutes, or until firm and golden. Cool on a wire rack. Sprinkle the orange slices with the icing sugar and grill (broil) until golden. Use to decorate the cake.

Cook's Tip

If you plan to keep the loaf for more than two or three days, omit the orange slices, brush with honey and sprinkle with flaked (sliced) hazelnuts.

Apple, Apricot and Walnut Loaf

This versatile recipe could also be made with pecan nuts, pears and plums. Serve slices of the loaf warm, and store what is left in an airtight tin.

1 Preheat the oven to 180°C/350°F/ Gas 4. Grease and line a 900g/2lb loaf tin (pan).

2 Sift the flour, baking powder and salt into a large mixing bowl, then tip the bran remaining in the sieve into the mixture. Add the margarine, sugar, eggs, orange rind and juice. Stir, then beat with a hand-held electric beater until smooth.

3 Stir in the walnuts and apricots. Add the apple to the mixture. Stir, then spoon into the tin and level the top.

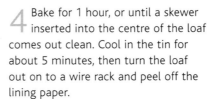

4 Bake for 1 hour, or until a skewer inserted into the centre of the loaf comes out clean. Cool in the tin for about 5 minutes, then turn the loaf out on to a wire rack and peel off the lining paper.

MAKES 1 LOAF

225g/8oz/2 cups plain (all-purpose) whole-
    meal (whole-wheat) flour
5ml/1 tsp baking powder
pinch of salt
115g/4oz/1/2 cup sunflower margarine
175g/6oz/3/4 cup soft light brown sugar
2 eggs, lightly beaten
grated rind and juice of 1 orange
50g/2oz/1/2 cup chopped walnuts
50g/2oz/1/4 cup ready-to-eat dried
    apricots, chopped
1 large cooking apple, peeled, quartered
    and chopped roughly

Nutritional information	
Calories	290kcal/1220kj
Fat	14.5g
Saturated fat	2.5g
Cholesterol	43.5mg
Fibre	1.6g

Banana and Ginger Teabread

Serve this teabread in slices with low-fat spread. The stem ginger adds an interesting flavour.

MAKES 1 LOAF

175g/6oz/1½ cups self-raising (self-rising) flour
5ml/1 tsp baking powder
40g/1½oz/3 tbsp soft margarine
50g/2oz/¼ cup dark muscovado (molasses) sugar
50g/2oz/¼ cup drained preserved stem ginger, chopped
60ml/4 tbsp skimmed milk
2 ripe bananas, mashed

Nutritional information	
Calories	214kcal/899kj
Fat	5.2g
Saturated fat	1g
Cholesterol	0.6mg
Fibre	1.6g

1 Preheat the oven to 180°C/350°F/ Gas 4. Grease and line a 450g/1lb loaf tin (pan). Sift the flour and baking powder into a mixing bowl.

2 Rub in the margarine until the mixture resembles breadcrumbs.

3 Stir in the sugar. Add the ginger, milk and bananas and mix to a soft dough.

4 Spoon into the tin and bake for 40–45 minutes. Run a metal spatula around the edges to loosen, then turn the teabread on to a wire rack and leave to cool.

Glazed Banana Spice Loaf

For an instant variation, omit the glaze and spread with quark for a tea-time treat.

1 Preheat the oven to 180°C/350°F/ Gas 4. Line a 23 x 13cm/9 x 5in loaf tin (pan) with greased baking parchment.

2 With a fork, mash the banana in a bowl. Set aside.

3 With an electric mixer, cream the butter and sugar until light and fluffy. Add the eggs, one at a time, beating to blend well after each addition. Sift together the flour, salt, bicarbonate of soda, nutmeg, allspice and cloves. Add to the butter mixture and stir to combine well.

4 Add the sour cream, banana and vanilla essence and mix just enough to blend. Pour into the prepared tin.

6 For the glaze, combine the icing sugar and lemon juice, then stir until smooth. To glaze, set the rack over a baking sheet. Pour the glaze over the top of the bread and allow to set.

MAKES 1 LOAF

1 large ripe banana
115g/4oz/½ cup butter
175g/6oz/scant 1 cup granulated sugar
2 eggs
175g/6oz/1½ cups plain
    (all-purpose) flour
5ml/1 tsp salt
5ml/1 tsp bicarbonate of soda
    (baking soda)
2.5ml/½ tsp freshly grated nutmeg
1.5ml/¼ tsp ground allspice
1.5ml/¼ tsp ground cloves
150ml/¼ pint/⅔ cup sour cream
5ml/1 tsp vanilla essence (extract)

For the glaze

175g/6oz/1 cup icing
    (confectioners') sugar
15–30ml/1–2 tbsp lemon juice

5 Bake for 45–50 minutes, until the top springs back when lightly touched. Allow to cool in the tin before turning out on to a wire rack.

Nutritional information	
Calories	362kcal/1522kj
Fat	14.1g
Saturated fat	4.3g
Cholesterol	49mg
Fibre	0.9g

Orange Honey Bread
A moist and fruity bread using naturally sweet ingredients.

MAKES 1 LOAF

275g/10oz/2½ cups plain
   (all-purpose) flour
12.5ml/2½ tsp baking powder
2.5ml/½ tsp bicarbonate of soda
   (baking soda)
2.5ml/½ tsp salt
30ml/2 tbsp margarine
350g/12oz/1¼ cups clear honey
1 egg, lightly beaten
25ml/1½ tbsp grated orange rind
175ml/6fl oz/¾cup freshly squeezed
   orange juice
75g/3oz/¾ cups chopped walnuts

Nutritional information

Calories	300kcal/1257kj
Fat	11.2g
Saturated fat	1.5g
Cholesterol	19.5mg
Fibre	1.6g

1 Preheat the oven to 160°C/325°F/
Gas 3. Sift together the flour, baking
powder, bicarbonate of soda and salt.

2 Line the bottom and sides of a
23 x 13cm/9 x 5in loaf tin (pan)
with greased baking parchment.

3 With an electric mixer, cream the
margarine until soft. Stir in the honey
until blended, then stir in the egg. Add
the orange rind and stir to combine.

4 Fold the flour mixture into the honey
and egg mixture in three batches,
alternating with the orange juice. Stir in
the walnuts.

5 Pour into the tin and bake for
60–70 minutes, or until a skewer
inserted into the centre comes out clean.
Allow to stand for 10 minutes before
turning on to a rack to cool.

Apple-sauce Bread

Apples and warm spices such as cinnamon and nutmeg are a perfect match in this tea bread.

1 Preheat the oven to 180°C/350°F/ Gas 4. Line the bottom and sides of a 23 x 13cm/9 x 5in loaf tin (pan) with greased baking parchment.

2 Break the egg into a bowl and beat lightly. Stir in the stewed apple, butter or margarine, and both sugars. Set aside.

3 In another bowl, sift together the flour, baking powder, bicarbonate of soda, salt, cinnamon and nutmeg. Fold the dry ingredients into the apple sauce mixture in three batches.

4 Stir in the currants or raisins and chopped pecan nuts.

5 Pour into the prepared tin and bake for about 1 hour, or until a skewer inserted in the centre comes out clean. Leave to stand for 10 minutes before transferring to a cooling rack.

MAKES 1 LOAF

1 egg
225g/8oz/1 cup stewed apple
50g/2oz/¼ cup butter or
   margarine, melted
75g/3oz/⅓ cup soft dark brown sugar
50g/2oz/¼ cup granulated sugar
225g/8oz/2 cups plain
   (all-purpose) flour
10ml/2 tsp baking powder
2.5ml/½ tsp bicarbonate of soda
   (baking soda)
2.5ml/½ tsp salt
5ml/1 tsp ground cinnamon
2.5ml/½ tsp freshly grated nutmeg
75g/3oz/½ cup currants or raisins
175g/6oz/1 cup pecan nuts, chopped

Nutritional information	
Calories	299kcal/1255kj
Fat	11.2g
Saturated fat	1.2g
Cholesterol	20mg
Fibre	1.8g

Cranberry Orange Bread

This classic muffin combination is equally delicious in this tasty teabread.

MAKES 1 LOAF

225g/8oz/2 cups plain
    (all-purpose) flour
115g/4oz/generous ½ cup caster
    (superfine) sugar
15ml/1 tbsp baking powder
2.5ml/½ tsp salt
grated rind of 1 large orange
150ml/¼ pint/⅔ cup fresh orange juice
2 eggs, lightly beaten
75g/3oz/6 tbsp butter or
    margarine, melted
175g/6oz/1½ cups fresh cranberries
50g/2oz/½ cup walnuts, chopped

Nutritional information

Calories	285kcal/1195kj
Fat	14g
Saturated fat	2.3g
Cholesterol	39mg
Fibre	2g

1 Preheat the oven to 180°C/350°F/ Gas 4. Line the bottom and sides of a 23 x 13cm/9 x 5in loaf tin (pan) with greased baking parchment. Sift the flour, sugar, baking powder and salt into a bowl.

2 Stir the grated orange rind into the dry ingredients.

3 Make a well in the centre of the dry ingredients and add the orange juice, eggs and melted butter or margarine. Stir from the centre until the ingredients are blended; do not overmix.

4 Add the cranberries and walnuts and stir well until blended. Transfer the batter to the prepared tin and bake for 45–50 minutes, or until a skewer inserted in the centre comes out clean.

5 Leave to cool in the tin for about 10 minutes before transferring to a rack to cool completely. Serve thinly sliced, toasted or plain, with butter.

Pear and Sultana Teabread

This is an ideal teabread to make when pears are plentiful – an excellent use for windfalls.

1 Preheat the oven to 180°C/350°F/ Gas 4. Grease and line a 450g/1lb loaf tin (pan) with baking parchment. Put the oats in a bowl with the sugar, pour over the pear or apple juice and oil, mix well and stand for 15 minutes.

2 Quarter, core and coarsely grate the pears. Add the fruit to the oat mixture with the flour, sultanas, baking powder, mixed spice and egg, then mix well.

3 Spoon the mixture into the prepared loaf tin and level the top. Bake for 50–60 minutes or until a skewer inserted into the centre comes out clean.

4 Transfer the teabread to a wire rack and peel off the lining paper. Leave to cool completely.

Cook's Tip

Health food shops sell concentrated pear and apple juice, ready for diluting as required.

MAKES 1 LOAF

25g/1oz/$\frac{1}{4}$ cup rolled oats
50g/2oz/$\frac{1}{4}$ cup light muscovado (brown) sugar
30ml/2 tbsp pear or apple juice
30ml/2 tbsp sunflower oil
1 large or 2 small pears
115g/4oz/1 cup self-raising (self-rising flour)
115g/4oz/$\frac{2}{3}$ cup sultanas (golden raisins)
2.5ml/$\frac{1}{2}$ tsp baking powder
10ml/2 tsp mixed (apple pie) spice
1 egg

Nutritional information	
Calories	200kcal/814kj
Fat	4.6g
Saturated fat	0.8g
Cholesterol	28mg
Fibre	1.4g

Dried Fruit Loaf

Dried fruit is a healthy sweet treat, and delicious in this loaf.

MAKES 1 LOAF

425g/15oz/2½ cups mixed dried fruit,
 such as currants, raisins, chopped
 dried apricots and dried cherries
300ml/½ pint/1¼ cups cold strong
 black tea
175g/6oz/¾ cup soft dark brown sugar
grated rind and juice of 1 small orange
grated rind and juice of 1 lemon
1 egg, lightly beaten
200g/7oz/1¾ cups plain
 (all-purpose) flour
15ml/1 tbsp baking powder
0.75ml/⅛ tsp salt

Nutritional information

Calories	298kcal/1252kj
Fat	1.1g
Saturated fat	0.2g
Cholesterol	19mg
Fibre	1.8g

1 In a bowl, toss together all the dried fruit, pour over the tea and leave to soak overnight.

2 Preheat the oven to 180°C/350°F/ Gas 4. Line the bottom and sides of a 23 x 13cm/9 x 5in loaf tin (pan) with greased baking parchment.

3 Strain the fruit, reserving the liquid. In a bowl, combine the sugar, orange and lemon rind and fruit.

4 Pour the orange and lemon juice into a measuring cup; if the quantity is less than 250ml/8fl oz/1 cup, make up with the soaking liquid.

5 Stir the citrus juices and egg into the dried fruit mixture.

6 In another bowl, sift together the flour, baking powder and salt. Stir into the fruit mixture until blended.

7 Transfer to the prepared tin and bake for 1¼ hours, or until a skewer inserted in the centre comes out clean. Allow to stand for 10 minutes before turning out.

Date and Nut Malt Loaf

This moist loaf is perfect for packed lunches.

1 Sift the flours and salt into a large bowl, adding any bran from the sieve. Stir in the sugar and yeast.

2 Put the butter or margarine in a small pan with the treacle and malt extract. Stir over a low heat until melted. Leave to cool, then mix in the milk.

3 Stir the liquid into the dry ingredients and knead thoroughly for 15 minutes until the dough is elastic. (If you have a dough blade on your food processor, follow the manufacturer's instructions for exact timings.)

4 Knead in the fruits and nuts. Transfer the dough to an oiled bowl, cover with clear film (plastic wrap), and leave in a warm place for about 1½ hours, until the dough has doubled in size.

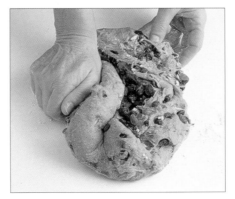

5 Grease two 450g/1lb loaf tins (pans). Knock back (punch down) the dough and knead lightly. Divide in half, form into loaves and place in the tins. Cover and leave in a warm place for about 30 minutes, until risen. Meanwhile, preheat the oven to 190°C/ 375°F/Gas 5.

6 Bake for 35–40 minutes, until well risen and sounding hollow when tapped underneath. Cool on a wire rack. Brush with 30ml/2 tbsp clear honey while warm to glaze, if you wish.

MAKES 2 LOAVES

300g/11oz/2⅔ cups strong white
    bread flour
275g/10oz/2½ cups strong wholemeal
    (whole-wheat) bread flour
5ml/1 tsp salt
75g/3oz/⅓ cup soft brown sugar
15ml/1 tsp easy-blend (rapid-rise)
    dried yeast
50g/2oz/¼ cup butter or margarine
15ml/1 tbsp black treacle (molasses)
60ml/4 tbsp malt extract
scant 250ml/8fl oz/1 cup tepid milk
115g/4oz/½ cup chopped dates
75g/3oz/½ cup sultanas (golden raisins)
75g/3oz/⅔ cup raisins
50g/2oz/½ cup chopped nuts

Nutritional information	
Calories	216kcal/907kj
Fat	5.6g
Saturated fat	2.5g
Cholesterol	9.5mg
Fibre	2.8g

Malt Loaf

This is a rich and sticky loaf. If it lasts long enough to go stale, try toasting it for an appetizing tea-time treat.

MAKES 1 LOAF

about 150ml/¼ pint/⅔ cup warm
skimmed milk
5ml/1 tsp active dried yeast
pinch of caster (superfine) sugar
350g/12oz/3 cups plain
    (all-purpose) flour
1.5ml/½ tsp salt
30ml/2 tbsp light muscovado
    (light brown) sugar
175g/6oz/1 cup sultanas
    (golden raisins)
15ml/1 tbsp sunflower oil
45ml/3 tbsp malt extract

For the glaze

30ml/2 tbsp caster (superfine) sugar
30ml/2 tbsp water

1 Place the warm milk in a bowl. Sprinkle the yeast on top and add the sugar. Leave for 30 minutes until frothy. Stir the flour and salt into a mixing bowl, stir in the muscovado sugar and sultanas, and make a well in the centre.

2 Add the yeast mixture with the oil and malt extract. Gradually add the flour and mix to a soft dough, adding a little extra milk if necessary.

3 Turn on to a floured surface and knead for about 5 minutes until smooth and elastic. Grease a 450g/1lb loaf tin (pan).

4 Shape the dough and place it in the loaf tin. Cover with a damp dishtowel and leave in a warm place for 1–2 hours until the dough is risen. Preheat the oven to 190°C/375°F/Gas 5.

5 Bake the loaf for 30–35 minutes, or until it sounds hollow when it is tapped underneath.

6 Meanwhile, prepare the glaze by dissolving the sugar in the water in a small pan. Bring to the boil, stirring, then lower the heat and simmer for 1 minute. Place the loaf on a wire rack and brush with the glaze while still hot. Leave the loaf to cool.

Variation

To make buns, divide the dough into ten pieces, shape into rounds, leave to rise, then bake for about 15–20 minutes. Brush with the glaze while still hot.

Nutritional information	
Calories	279kcal/1171kj
Fat	2.1g
Saturated fat	0.3g
Cholesterol	0.4mg
Fibre	1.8g

Lemon Walnut Bread

This is a light and tangy teabread, with an agreeable crunchiness from the nuts.

MAKES 1 LOAF

115g/4oz/½ cup butter or margarine
115g/4oz/generous ½ cup caster
   (superfine) sugar
2 eggs, separated
grated rind of 2 lemons
30ml/2 tbsp fresh lemon juice
175g/6oz/1½ cups self-raising
   (self-rising) flour
10ml/2 tsp baking powder
120ml/4fl oz/½ cup milk
175g/6oz/1½ cups chopped walnuts
0.75ml/⅛ tsp salt

Nutritional information	
Calories	229kcal/962kj
Fat	11.1g
Saturated fat	1.8g
Cholesterol	39mg
Fibre	1g

1 Preheat the oven to 180°C/350°F/ Gas 4. Line the bottom and sides of a 23 x 13cm/9 x 5in loaf tin (pan) with baking parchment and grease.

2 With an electric mixer, cream the butter or margarine with the sugar until light and fluffy.

3 Beat the egg yolks into the creamed butter and sugar.

4 Add the lemon rind and juice and stir until blended. Set aside.

5 In another bowl, sift together the flour and baking powder, three times. Fold into the butter mixture in three batches, alternating with the milk. Fold in the chopped walnuts and set aside.

6 Beat the egg whites and salt until stiff peaks form. Fold a large dollop of the egg whites into the walnut mixture to lighten it. Fold in the remaining egg whites carefully until just blended.

7 Pour the batter into the tin, bake for 45–50 minutes. Leave to stand for 5 minutes before turning on to a rack to cool completely.

Apricot Nut Loaf

The combination of dried fruits and nuts provides high fibre in this tea bread.

1 Preheat the oven to 180°C/350°F/ Gas 4. Line the bottom and sides of a 23 x 13cm/9 x 5in loaf tin (pan) with baking parchment and grease.

2 Place the apricots in a bowl and add lukewarm water to cover. Allow to stand for 30 minutes.

3 With a vegetable peeler, remove the orange rind, leaving the pith. With a sharp knife, finely chop the orange rind strips.

4 Drain the apricots and chop coarsely. Place in a bowl with the orange rind and raisins. Set aside. Squeeze the peeled orange. Measure the juice and add enough hot water to make 175ml/6fl oz/ ¾ cup liquid.

5 Pour the orange juice mixture over the apricot mixture. Stir in the sugar, oil and eggs. Set aside.

6 In another bowl, sift together the flour, baking powder, salt and bicarbonate of soda. Fold the flour mixture into the apricot mixture in three batches.

7 Stir in the walnuts. Spoon the batter into the prepared tin and bake for about 55–60 minutes, or until a skewer inserted in the centre of the loaf comes out clean. If the loaf browns too quickly, protect the top with foil. Cool in the tin for 10 minutes before transferring to a rack to cool completely.

MAKES 1 LOAF

175g/6oz/¾ cup dried apricots
1 large orange
75g/3oz/⅔ cup raisins
150g/5oz/¾ cup caster (superfine) sugar
90ml/3fl oz/⅓ cup oil
2 eggs, lightly beaten
250g/9oz/2½ cups plain (all-purpose) flour
10ml/2 tsp baking powder
2.5ml/½ tsp salt
5ml/1 tsp bicarbonate soda (baking soda)
50g/2oz/½ cup chopped walnuts

Nutritional information

Calories	324kcal/1365kj
Fat	11.2g
Saturated fat	1.5g
Cholesterol	38mg
Fibre	2.5g

Date-nut Bread

Adding a little brandy to this teabread provides an extra rich flavour.

MAKES 1 LOAF

150g/5oz/1¼ cups pitted
   dates, chopped
175ml/6fl oz/¾ cup boiling water
60ml/4 tbsp unsalted butter
40g/1½oz/scant ¼ cup soft dark
   brown sugar
50g/2oz/¼ cup caster (superfine) sugar
1 egg
30ml/2 tbsp brandy
165g/5½oz/1⅓ cups plain
(all-purpose) flour
10ml/2 tsp baking powder
2.5ml/½ tsp salt
generous 2.5ml/½ tsp freshly
   grated nutmeg
75g/3oz/¾ cup pecan nuts, coarsely chopped

Nutritional information	
Calories	258kcal/1077kj
Fat	13.8g
Saturated fat	1.1g
Cholesterol	20mg
Fibre	1.3g

1 Place the dates in a bowl and pour over the boiling water. Set aside to cool until lukewarm.

2 Preheat the oven to 180°C/350°F/ Gas 4. Line the bottom and sides of a 23 x 13cm/9 x 5in loaf tin (pan) with baking parchment and grease.

3 With an electric mixer, cream the butter and sugars until they are light and fluffy. Beat in the egg and brandy, then set aside.

4 Sift the flour, baking powder, salt and nutmeg together, three times.

5 Fold the dry ingredients into the sugar mixture in three batches, alternating with the dates and water.

6 Fold in the pecan nuts. Pour the batter into the prepared tin and bake for 45–50 minutes, or until a skewer inserted in the centre comes out clean. Cool in the pan for 10 minutes before transferring to a rack to cool completely.

Prune Bread

A slightly spicy bread that tastes good with savoury spreads.

1 Simmer the prunes in water to cover until soft, or soak overnight. Drain, reserving 50ml/2fl oz/¼ cup of the soaking liquid. Pit and chop the prunes.

2 Combine the yeast and the reserved prune liquid, stir, and leave for 15 minutes to dissolve.

3 In a large bowl, stir together the flours, bicarbonate of soda, salt and pepper. Make a well in the centre.

4 Add the chopped prunes, butter and buttermilk. Pour in the yeast mixture. With a wooden spoon, stir from the centre, incorporating more flour with each turn, to obtain a rough dough.

5 Transfer to a floured surface and knead until smooth and elastic. Return to the clean bowl, cover with a plastic bag, and leave to rise in a warm place until doubled in volume, for about 1½ hours. Grease a baking sheet.

6 Knock back (punch down) the dough with your fist, then knead in the chopped walnuts.

7 Shape the dough into a long, cylindrical loaf. Place on the baking sheet, cover loosely, and leave to rise in a warm place for 45 minutes.

8 Preheat the oven to 220°C/425°F/ Gas 7. With a sharp knife, score the top deeply. Brush with milk and bake for 15 minutes. Lower the heat to 190°C/ 375°F/Gas 5 and bake for 35 minutes more, until the bottom sounds hollow when tapped. Cool on a rack.

MAKES 1 LOAF

225g/8oz/1 cup prunes
10ml/2 tsp active dried yeast
50g/2oz/½ cup strong wholemeal (whole-wheat) bread flour
275–350g/10–12oz/2½–3 cups strong white bread flour
2.5ml/½ tsp bicarbonate of soda (baking soda)
5ml/1 tsp salt
5ml/1 tsp ground black pepper
30ml/2 tbsp butter
175ml/6fl oz/¾ cup buttermilk
175g/6oz/1 cup walnuts, chopped

Nutritional information	
Calories	262kcal/1104kj
Fat	8.4g
Saturated fat	1.1g
Cholesterol	1mg
Fibre	2.1g

Swedish Fruit Bread

A lightly sweetened fruit bread that is good served warm. It is also excellent toasted and topped with low-fat spread.

MAKES 1 LOAF

150ml/¼ pint/⅔ cup lukewarm water

5ml/1 tsp active dried yeast

15ml/1 tbsp clear honey

225g/8oz/2 cups strong wholemeal (whole-wheat) bread flour

225g/8oz/2 cups strong white bread flour

5ml/1 tsp salt

115g/4oz/⅔ cup sultanas (golden raisins)

50g/2oz/⅓ cup walnuts, finely chopped

175ml/6fl oz/¾ cup warm skimmed milk, plus extra for glazing

Variation

To make Apple and Hazelnut Bread, replace the sultanas with two chopped eating apples and use chopped toasted hazelnuts instead of the walnuts. Add 5ml/1 tsp ground cinnamon with the flour.

Nutritional information	
Calories	273kcal/1145kj
Fat	4.86g
Saturated fat	0.57g
Cholesterol	0.4mg
Fibre	3.8g

1 Put the water in a small jug. Sprinkle the yeast on top. Add a few drops of the honey to help activate the yeast, mix well and leave to stand for 10 minutes.

2 Put the flours in a mixing bowl, with the salt and sultanas. Set aside 15ml/1 tbsp of the walnuts and add the rest to the bowl. Mix together lightly and make a well in the centre.

3 Add the yeast and honey mixture to the flour mixture with the milk and remaining honey. Gradually incorporate the flour, mixing to a soft dough; add a little extra water if the dough feels too dry to work with.

4 Turn the dough on to a floured surface and knead for 5 minutes until smooth and elastic. Return to the clean bowl, cover with a damp dishtowel and leave in a warm place to rise for about 2 hours until doubled in bulk. Grease a baking sheet.

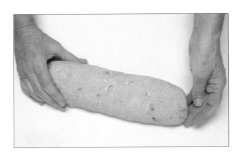

5 Turn the dough on to a floured surface and form into a 28cm/11in long sausage shape. Place on the baking sheet. Make some diagonal cuts down the whole length of the loaf.

6 Brush the loaf with milk, sprinkle with the reserved walnuts and leave to rise for about 40 minutes. Preheat the oven to 220°C/425°F/Gas 7. Bake for 10 minutes. Lower the temperature to 200°C/400°F/Gas 6 and bake for about 20 minutes more, or until the loaf sounds hollow when tapped.

Raisin Bread

Spice, brandy and dried fruit make a good flavour combination.

MAKES 2 LOAVES

10ml/2 tsp dried yeast
475ml/16fl oz/2 cups lukewarm milk
175g/6oz/1¼ cups raisins
65g/2½oz/¼ cup currants
15ml/1 tbsp sherry or brandy
2.5ml/½ tsp freshly grated nutmeg
grated rind of 1 large orange
75g/3oz/6 tbsp caster (superfine) sugar
15ml/1 tbsp salt
115g/4oz/½ cup butter, melted
500–675g/1¼–1½ lb/5–6 cups
    strong white bread flour
1 egg beaten with 15ml/1 tbsp cream,
to glaze

Nutritional information

Calories	235kcal/994kj
Fat	5.9g
Saturated fat	1.2g
Cholesterol	11mg
Fibre	1.4g

1 Stir together the yeast and 120ml/ 4fl oz/½ cup of the milk and leave to stand for 15 minutes to dissolve.

2 Mix the raisins, currants, sherry or brandy, nutmeg and orange rind together and set aside.

3 In another bowl, mix the remaining milk, sugar, salt and 50g/2oz/¼ cup of the butter. Add the yeast mixture. With a wooden spoon, stir in 225–275g/ 8–10oz/2–3 cups flour, 115g/4oz/1 cup at a time, until blended. Add more flour for a stiff dough.

4 Transfer to a floured surface and knead until smooth and elastic. Place in a greased bowl, cover, and leave to rise in a warm place until doubled in volume, for about 2½ hours.

5 Knock back (punch down) the dough, return to the bowl, cover, and leave to rise in a warm place for 30 minutes.

6 Grease two 23 x 13cm/9 x 5in bread tins (pans). Divide the dough in half and roll each half into a rectangle about 50 x 18cm/20 x 7in.

7 Brush the rectangles with the remaining melted butter. Sprinkle over the raising mixture, then roll up tightly from the short end, tucking in the ends slightly as you roll. Place in the prepared tins, cover and leave to rise until almost doubled in volume.

8 Preheat the oven to 200°C/400°F/ Gas 6. Brush the top of the loaves with the glaze. Bake for 20 minutes. Lower the heat to 180°C/350°F/Gas 4 and bake for 25–30 minutes more, or until golden. Cool on racks.

Sweet Potato and Raisin Bread

The natural sweetness of sweet potato is used in this healthy loaf.

1 Preheat the oven to 180°C/350°F/ Gas 4. Grease a 23 x 13cm/9 x 5in loaf tin (pan).

2 Sift the flour, baking powder, salt, cinnamon and nutmeg into a small bowl. Set aside.

3 With an electric mixer, beat the mashed sweet potatoes with the brown sugar, butter or margarine and eggs until well mixed.

4 Add the flour mixture and the raisins. Stir with a wooden spoon until the flour is just mixed in.

5 Transfer the batter to the prepared tin. Bake for 1–1¼ hours, or until a skewer inserted in the centre comes out clean.

6 Cool in the pan on a wire rack for 15 minutes, then turn the bread on to a wire rack and cool completely.

MAKES 1 LOAF

225–275g/8–10oz/2–2½ cups
  plain (all-purpose) flour
10ml/2 tsp baking powder
2.5ml/½ tsp salt
5ml/1 tsp ground cinnamon
2.5ml/½ tsp freshly grated nutmeg
450g/1lb/5 cups cooked mashed
  sweet potatoes
75g/3oz/⅓ cup soft light brown sugar
115g/4oz/½ cup butter or margarine,
  melted and cooled
3 eggs, beaten
75g/3oz/generous ½ cup raisins

Nutritional information	
Calories	338kcal/1420kj
Fat	11.6g
Saturated fat	2.4g
Cholesterol	59mg
Fibre	2.4g

Cardamom and Saffron Tealoaf

This aromatic sweet bread is ideal for afternoon tea or lightly toasted for breakfast.

MAKES 1 LOAF

good pinch of saffron threads
750ml/1¼ pints/3 cups lukewarm milk
25g/1oz/2 tbsp butter
900g/2lb/8 cups strong white
    bread flour
10ml/2 tsp easy-blend (rapid-rise)
    dried yeast
40g/1½oz caster (superfine) sugar
6 cardamom pods, split open and
    seeds extracted
115g/4oz/⅔ cup raisins
30ml/2 tbsp clear honey
1 egg, beaten

Nutritional information

Calories	226kcal/952kj
Fat	2.1g
Saturated fat	0.4g
Cholesterol	10mg
Fibre	1.7g

1 Crush the saffron into a cup containing a little of the warm milk and leave to infuse for 5 minutes.

2 Rub the butter into the flour, then mix in the yeast, sugar and cardamom seeds (these may need rubbing to separate them). Stir in the raisins.

3 Beat the remaining milk with the honey and egg, then mix this into the flour with the saffron milk and threads, stirring well until a firm dough is formed. You may not need all the milk; it depends on the flour.

4 Turn out the dough and knead it on a lightly floured board for about 5 minutes until smooth.

5 Return the dough to the mixing bowl, cover with oiled clear film (plastic wrap) and leave in a warm place until doubled in size. Grease a 900g/2lb loaf tin (pan). Turn the dough out on to a floured board again, knock it back (punch it down), knead for three minutes, then shape it into a fat roll and fit it into the greased loaf tin.

6 Cover with a sheet of lightly oiled clear film and stand in a warm place until the dough begins to rise again. Preheat the oven to 200°C/400°F/Gas 6. Bake the loaf for 25 minutes until golden brown and firm on top. Turn out of the tin and, as it cools, brush the top with honey. Slice when cold and spread with butter. It is also good lightly toasted.

Sweet Sesame Loaf

Toasted sesame seeds add a lovely nutty flavour to this loaf.

1 Preheat the oven to 180°C/350°F/ Gas 4. Line a 25 x 15cm/10 x 6in baking tin (pan), or two small loaf tins (pans), with greased baking parchment.

2 Reserve 30ml/2 tbsp of the sesame seeds. Spread the rest on a baking sheet and bake until lightly toasted, for about 10 minutes. Sift the flour, baking powder and salt into a bowl.

3 Stir in the toasted sesame seeds and set aside. With an electric mixer, cream the butter or margarine and sugar together until light and fluffy. Beat in the eggs, then stir in the lemon rind and milk.

4 Pour the milk mixture over the dry ingredients and fold in with a large metal spoon until just blended.

5 Pour into the pan and sprinkle over the reserved sesame seeds.

6 Bake for about 1 hour, or until a skewer inserted into the centre comes out clean. Cool in the pan for 10 minutes before turning out.

MAKES 1 LARGE OR 2 SMALL LOAVES

150g/5oz/1¼ cups sesame seeds
225g/8oz/2 cups plain
   (all-purpose) flour
12.5ml/2½ tsp baking powder
5ml/1 tsp salt
60ml/4 tbsp butter or margarine
150g/5oz/¾ cup caster
   (superfine) sugar
2 eggs
grated rind of 1 lemon
350ml/12fl oz/1½ cups milk

Nutritional information

Calories	133kcal/562kj
Fat	5.1g
Saturated fat	0.9g
Cholesterol	20mg
Fibre	0.7g

Greek Easter Bread

In Greece, this traditional bread, decorated with red dyed eggs, is made during Easter celebrations.

MAKES 1 LOAF

25g/1oz fresh yeast

120ml/4fl oz/½ cup warm milk

675g/1½lb/6 cups strong white
    bread flour

2 eggs, beaten

2.5ml/½ tsp caraway seeds

15ml/1 tbsp caster (superfine) sugar

15ml/1 tbsp brandy

50g/2oz/¼ cup butter, melted

1 egg white, beaten

50g/2oz/½ cup split almonds

2–3 hard-boiled eggs, dyed red

Nutritional information

Calories	344kcal/1453kj
Fat	10.1g
Saturated fat	3.6g
Cholesterol	89mg
Fibre	2.5g

1 Crumble the yeast into a bowl. Mix with 15–30ml/1–2 tbsp of warm water, until softened. Add the milk and 115g/4oz/1 cup of the flour and mix to a creamy consistency. Cover with a cloth, and leave in a warm place to rise for 1 hour.

2 Sift the remaining flour into a bowl and make a well in the centre. Pour the risen yeast into the well, and draw in a little of the flour from the sides. Add the eggs, caraway seeds, sugar and brandy. Add the remaining flour until the mixture begins to form a dough.

3 Mix in the melted butter. Turn on to a floured surface and knead for about 10 minutes, until the dough becomes smooth. Return to the bowl and cover with a damp dishtowel. Leave in a warm place for 3 hours.

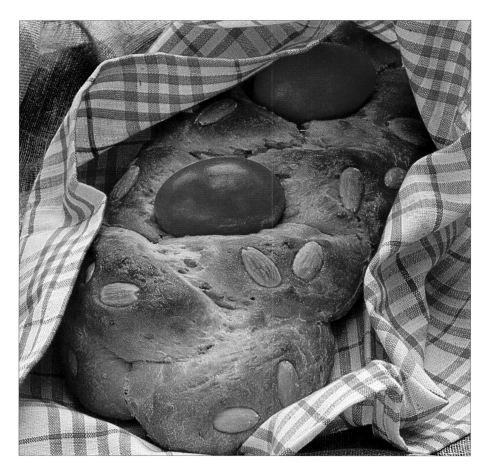

4 Preheat the oven to 180°C/350°F/ Gas 4. Knock back (punch down) the dough, turn on to a floured surface and knead for a minute or two. Divide the dough into three and roll each piece into a long sausage shape. Make a braid as shown above and place the loaf on a greased baking sheet.

5 Tuck the ends under, brush with the egg white and decorate with the split almonds. Bake for about 1 hour, until the loaf sounds hollow when tapped underneath. Cool on a wire rack. Serve decorated with the hard-boiled eggs.

Orange Wheat Loaf

Perfect just with butter as a breakfast bread or teabread and lovely for banana sandwiches.

1 Sift the flour into a large bowl and return any wheat flakes from the sieve. Add the salt and rub in the butter lightly with your fingertips.

2 Stir in the sugar, yeast and orange rind. Pour the orange juice into a measuring jug (cup) and make up to 200ml/7fl oz/scant 1 cup with hot (not more than hand hot) water.

3 Stir the liquid into the flour and mix to a soft ball of dough. Knead the dough gently on a lightly floured surface until quite smooth.

4 Place the dough in a greased 450g/ 1lb loaf tin (pan) and leave in a warm place until nearly doubled in size. Preheat the oven to 220°C/425°F/Gas 7.

5 Bake the bread for 30–35 minutes, or until it sounds hollow when you tap the loaf underneath. Tip out of the tin and cool on a wire rack.

MAKES 1 LOAF

275g/10 oz/2½ cups plain (all-purpose) wholemeal (whole-wheat) flour
2.5ml/½ tsp salt
50g/2oz/¼ cup butter
25g/1oz/2 tbsp soft light brown sugar
½ sachet easy-blend (rapid-rise) dried yeast
grated rind and juice of ½ orange

Nutritional information

Calories	144kcal/607kj
Fat	3.3g
Saturated fat	1.8g
Cholesterol	7.2mg
Fibre	3.2g

SAVOURY BAKES

Pizzas, mini tarts, frittatas, pies and parcels are all delicious for a
quick snack or light lunch. Popovers and wholemeal herb
triangles are quick and easy to make; both make a tasty
addition to serve with roast meat or chicken.

Smoked Salmon Pizzettes

Mini-pizzas, when topped with smoked salmon, crème fraîche and lumpfish roe make extra special party canapés.

MAKES 10–12

150g/5oz packet of pizza dough mix
15ml/1 tbsp chopped
fresh chives
15ml/1 tbsp olive oil
75–115g/3–4oz smoked salmon,
    cut into strips
60ml/4 tbsp crème fraîche
30ml/2 tbsp black lumpfish roe
chives, to garnish

Nutritional information

Calories	126kcal/532kj
Fat	2.9g
Saturated fat	0.8g
Cholesterol	37mg
Fibre	0.9g

1 Preheat the oven to 200°C/400°F/ Gas 6. Grease two baking sheets. Knead the dough gently, adding the chives until evenly mixed.

2 Roll out the dough on a lightly floured surface to about 3mm/⅛in thick. Using a 7.5cm/3in plain round cutter, stamp out 10–12 rounds.

3 Place the bases well apart on the two baking sheets, prick all over with a fork, then brush with the oil. Bake for 10–15 minutes until crisp and golden.

4 Arrange the smoked salmon on top, then spoon on the crème fraîche. Spoon a tiny amount of lumpfish roe in the centre and garnish with chives. Serve immediately.

Calzone

This pizza looks rather like a large turnover; it is folded in half to enclose the filling. Because they are so portable, they are eaten as street food in Italy.

1 To make the dough, sift the flour and salt into a bowl and stir in the yeast. Stir in just enough warm water to make a soft dough.

2 Knead for 5 minutes until smooth. Cover and leave in a warm place for about 1 hour, or until doubled in size.

3 Meanwhile, to make the filling, heat the oil and sauté the onion and courgettes for 3–4 minutes. Remove from the heat and add the tomatoes, cheese, oregano and seasoning.

4 Preheat the oven to 220°C/425°F/ Gas 7. Knead the dough lightly and divide into four. Roll out each piece on a lightly floured surface to a 20cm/8in round and place a quarter of the filling on one half of each round.

5 Brush the edges with milk and fold over to enclose the filling. Press firmly to enclose. Brush with milk.

6 Bake on an oiled baking sheet for 15–20 minutes. Serve hot or cold.

SERVES 4

450g/1lb/4 cups strong white
    bread flour
pinch of salt
10ml/2 tsp easy-blend (rapid-rise)
    dried yeast
350ml/12fl oz/1½ cups warm water

For the filling

5ml/1 tsp olive oil
1 medium red onion, thinly sliced
3 medium courgettes (zucchini), sliced
2 large tomatoes, diced
150g/5oz mozzarella cheese, diced
15ml/1 tbsp chopped fresh oregano
salt and ground black pepper
skimmed milk, to glaze

Nutritional information	
Calories	544kcal/2885kj
Fat	10.9g
Saturated fat	5.5g
Cholesterol	24.4mg
Fibre	5.1g

Fresh Herb Pizza

Cut this pizza into thin wedges and serve as part of a mixed antipasti.

SERVES 8

115g/4oz mixed fresh herbs, such as
    parsley, basil and oregano
3 garlic cloves, crushed
120ml/4fl oz/½ cup double
    (heavy) cream
1 pizza base, 25–30cm/
    10–12in diameter
15ml/1 tbsp garlic oil
115g/4oz/1 cup grated Pecorino cheese
salt and ground black pepper

Nutritional information

Calories	219kcal/913kj
Fat	8.1g
Saturated fat	3.4g
Cholesterol	27mg
Fibre	1g

1 Preheat the oven to 220°C/425°F/ Gas 7. Chop the herbs, using a food processor if you have one.

2 In a bowl, mix together the herbs, garlic, cream and seasoning.

3 Brush the pizza base with the garlic oil, then spread over the herb and garlic mixture.

4 Sprinkle over the Pecorino cheese. Bake for 15–20 minutes until crisp and golden and the topping is still moist. Cut into thin wedges to serve.

Mini pizzas

For a quick supper, try these delicious little pizzas made with fresh and sun-dried tomatoes.

1 Preheat the oven to 200°C/400°F/ Gas 6. Make up the pizza base following the instructions on the side of the packet.

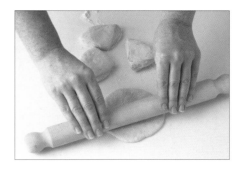

2 Divide the dough into four and roll each piece out to a 13cm/5in round. Place on two lightly oiled baking sheets.

3 Place the sun-dried tomatoes and olives in a blender or food processor and blend until smooth. Spread the mixture evenly over the pizza bases.

Cook's Tip

You could use loose sun-dried tomatoes (preserved without oil) if you wish. Leave in a bowl of warm water for 10–15 minutes to soften, drain and blend with the olives.

4 Top with the tomato slices and crumble over the goat's cheese. Bake for 10–15 minutes. Sprinkle with the fresh basil and serve at once.

MAKES 4

150g/5oz packet of pizza dough mix
8 halves sun-dried tomatoes in olive oil, drained
50g/2oz/½ cup pitted black olives
1 ripe beefsteak tomato, sliced
50g/2oz/¼ cup goat's cheese
30ml/2 tbsp fresh basil leaves

Nutritional information	
Calories	326kcal/1369kj
Fat	11.3g
Saturated fat	2.8g
Cholesterol	34mg
Fibre	2.8g

Spinach and Feta Triangles

Feta is a medium-fat cheese with a tangy, slightly salty flavour.

MAKES 20

30ml/2 tbsp olive oil
2 shallots, finely chopped
450g/1lb/3 cups frozen
    spinach, thawed
115g/4oz/1 cup crumbled feta cheese
25g/1oz/2 tbsp walnut pieces, chopped
1.5ml/¼ tsp freshly grated nutmeg
4 large or 8 small sheets filo pastry,
    thawed if frozen
50g/2oz/¼ cup butter or
    margarine, melted
salt and ground black pepper

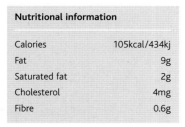

Variation

For an alternative filling, omit the spinach and shallots. Use 350g/12oz/1½ cups crumbled goat's cheese, instead of the feta cheese, and 50g/2oz/½ cup toasted pine nuts instead of the walnuts. Mix the cheese with the olive oil and 15ml/1 tbsp chopped fresh basil. Assemble as above.

Nutritional information	
Calories	105kcal/434kj
Fat	9g
Saturated fat	2g
Cholesterol	4mg
Fibre	0.6g

1 Preheat the oven to 200°C/400°F/ Gas 6.

2 Heat the olive oil in a skillet. Add the shallots and cook until softened, for about 5 minutes.

3 A handful at a time, squeeze all the liquid out of the spinach. Add the spinach to the shallots. Increase the heat to high and cook, stirring, until all the excess moisture has evaporated, for about 5 minutes.

4 Transfer the spinach mixture to a bowl. Cool. Stir in the feta and walnuts. Season with nutmeg, salt and pepper.

5 Lay a filo sheet on a flat surface. (Keep the remaining filo covered with a damp cloth to prevent it drying out.) Brush with some of the butter or margarine. Lay a second filo sheet on top of the first. With scissors, cut the layered filo pastry lengthways into 7.5cm/3in wide strips.

6 Place 15ml/1tbsp of the spinach mixture at the end of one strip of filo pastry.

7 Fold a bottom corner of the pastry over the filling to form a triangle, then continue folding over the pastry strip to the other end. Fill and shape the triangles until all the ingredients are used.

8 Set the triangles on baking sheets and brush with butter. Bake the filo triangles until they are crispy and golden brown, for about 10 minutes. Serve hot.

Salmon Parcels

Serve these little savoury parcels just as they are for a snack, or with a pool of fresh tomato sauce for a special starter.

3 Place a single sheet of filo pastry on a work surface and brush lightly with oil. Then place another sheet on top. Cut into six squares, about 10cm/4in. Repeat with the remaining pastry, to make 12 squares.

4 Place a spoonful of the salmon mixture on to each square. Brush the edges of the pastry with oil, then draw together as shown above, pressing to seal.

5 Place the pastries on a baking sheet and bake for 12–15 minutes, until golden. Serve warm, with spring onions and salad leaves.

MAKES 12

90g/3½oz can red or pink salmon
15ml/1 tbsp chopped fresh
    coriander (cilantro)
4 spring onions (scallions),
    finely chopped
4 sheets filo pastry, thawed if frozen
sunflower oil, for brushing
spring onions and salad leaves,
    to serve

Nutritional information

Calories	25kcal/1074kj
Fat	1.2g
Saturated fat	0.2g
Cholesterol	2.6mg
Fibre	0.1g

1 Preheat the oven to 200°C/400°F/ Gas 6. Lightly oil a baking sheet. Drain the salmon, discarding any skin and bones, then place in a bowl.

2 Flake the salmon with a fork and then mix with the fresh coriander and spring onions.

Cook's Tip

When you are using filo pastry, it is important to prevent it drying out; cover any you are not using with a dish towel or clear film (plastic wrap).

Tomato Cheese Tarts

These crisp little tartlets are simple to make and quick to cook. They are at their best when served fresh from the oven. Add a salad or soup for a tasty lunch or snack.

SERVES 4

2 sheets filo pastry, thawed if frozen
1 egg white
115g/4oz/½ cup skimmed-
    milk soft cheese
handful of fresh basil leaves
3 small tomatoes, sliced
salt and ground black pepper

Nutritional information	
Calories	50kcal/210kj
Fat	0.3g
Saturated fat	0.1g
Cholesterol	0.3mg
Fibre	0.3g

1 Preheat the oven to 200°C/400°F/ Gas 6. Brush the sheets of filo pastry lightly with egg white and cut into sixteen 10cm/4in squares.

3 Arrange the tomato slices on the tarts, add seasoning and bake for 10–12 minutes, until golden. Serve the tarts warm.

2 Layer the squares in twos, in eight patty tins (muffin pans). Spoon the cheese into the pastry cases. Season with black pepper and top with basil leaves.

Red Pepper and Watercress Filo Parcels

Peppery watercress combines well with sweet red pepper in these crisp little parcels.

MAKES 8

3 red (bell) peppers
175g/6oz/1 bunch watercress or
   rocket (arugula)
225g/8oz/1 cup ricotta cheese
50g/2oz/⅓ cup blanched almonds,
   toasted and chopped
8 sheets filo pastry, thawed if frozen
30ml/2 tbsp olive oil
salt and ground black pepper

1 Preheat the oven to 190°C/375°F/ Gas 5. Place the peppers under a hot grill until blistered and charred. Place in a plastic bag. When cool enough to handle, peel, seed and pat dry on kitchen paper.

4 Working with one sheet of filo pastry at a time, cut out two 18cm/7in and two 5cm/2in squares from each sheet. Brush one large square with a little olive oil and place a second large square at an angle of 90 degrees to form a star shape.

2 Place the peppers and watercress or rocket in a food processor and blend until coarsely chopped. Spoon into a bowl.

5 Place one of the small squares in the centre of the star shape, brush lightly with oil and top with a second small square.

Variation

Instead of using watercress or rocket (arugula), try using spinach. Add a pinch of nutmeg, a squeeze of lemon juice and some freshly chopped mint.

3 Mix in the ricotta and almonds, and season to taste.

6 Top with one-eighth of the red pepper mixture. Bring the edges together to form a purse shape and twist to seal. Place on a greased baking sheet and cook for 25–30 minutes until golden.

Nutritional information

Calories	168kcal/699kj
Fat	10.2g
Saturated fat	2.7g
Cholesterol	14mg
Fibre	1.7g

Spinach and Cheese Pie

Low-fat cottage cheese cuts calories in this delicious pie, and Parmesan cheese adds flavour.

1 Preheat the oven to 190°C/375°F/ Gas 5.

2 Stack handfuls of spinach leaves, roll them loosely, and cut across the leaves into thin ribbons. Heat the oil in a large pan. Add the onion and cook until softened, for about 5 minutes.

3 Add the spinach and oregano and cook for about 5 minutes over a high heat until most of the liquid from the spinach evaporates, stirring frequently. Remove from the heat and allow to cool. Break the eggs into a bowl and beat until mixed together. Stir in the cottage cheese and Parmesan cheese and season generously with nutmeg, salt and pepper. Stir in the spinach mixture.

4 Brush a 33 x 23cm/13 x 9in baking dish with some of the butter or margarine. Arrange half of the filo sheets in the bottom of the dish to cover evenly and extend about 2.5cm/1in up the sides. Brush with butter.

5 Ladle in the spinach and cheese filling. Cover with the remaining filo pastry, tucking under the edge neatly.

6 Brush the top with the remaining butter. Score the top with diamond shapes using a sharp knife.

7 Bake for about 30 minutes, or until the pastry is golden brown. Cut the pie into eight squares and serve while it is still hot.

SERVES 8

1.3g/3lb fresh spinach, coarse stems removed
30ml/2 tbsp olive oil
1 medium onion, finely chopped
30ml/2 tbsp chopped fresh oregano or 5ml/1 tsp dried oregano
4 eggs
225g/8oz/1 cup creamed low-fat cottage cheese
90ml/6 tbsp freshly grated Parmesan cheese
freshly grated nutmeg
50g/2oz/¼ cup butter or margarine, melted
12 sheets filo pasty, thawed if frozen
salt and ground black pepper

Nutritional information

Calories	299kcal/1244kj
Fat	16.4g
Saturated fat	4.4g
Cholesterol	105mg
Fibre	3.8g

Celeriac Gratin

Celeriac is a vegetable with a sweet and nutty flavour, which is accentuated by the cheese in this dish.

SERVES 4

450g/1lb celeriac
juice of ½ lemon
25g/1oz/2 tbsp butter or margarine
1 small onion, finely chopped
30ml/2 tbsp plain (all-purpose) flour
300ml/½ pint/1¼ cups skimmed milk
25g/1oz/¼ cup grated
   Emmenthal cheese
15ml/1 tbsp capers
salt and cayenne pepper

1 Preheat the oven to 190°C/375°F/ Gas 5. Peel the celeriac and cut into 5mm/¼in slices, immediately plunging them into a pan of cold water acidulated with the lemon juice.

2 Bring the water to the boil and simmer the celeriac for 10–12 minutes until just tender. Drain and arrange the celeriac in a shallow ovenproof dish.

3 Melt the butter in a small pan and fry the onion over a gentle heat until soft but not browned. Stir in the flour, cook for 1 minute, then stir in the milk to make a smooth sauce. Stir in the cheese, capers and seasoning to taste, then pour over the celeriac. Cook in the oven for 15–20 minutes, or until golden brown.

Cook's Tip

For a less strongly flavoured dish, alternate the layers of celeriac with potato. Slice the potato, cook until almost tender, drain then assemble the dish.

Nutritional information

Calories	146kcal/616kj
Fat	7.7g
Saturated fat	2.2g
Cholesterol	8mg
Fibre	4.7g

Carrot Soufflés

Use tender young carrots for this light-as-air dish.

SERVES 4

450g/1lb carrots
4 eggs, separated
30ml/2 tbsp chopped fresh
    coriander (cilantro)
salt and ground black pepper

Cook's Tips

Fresh coriander (cilantro) tastes wonderful and it's well worth growing your own coriander plant in a window box to ensure a regular supply. It is also available freeze-dried in some supermarkets – although less impressive than the fresh variety, it is a better alternative than dried herbs.

Baked soufflés are quite delicate; once the hot air escapes, they will deflate quickly, so as soon as you take them out of the oven, serve them at once, while they are still well risen.

Nutritional information

Calories	115kcal/481kj
Fat	5.8g
Saturated fat	1.6g
Cholesterol	193mg
Fibre	2.7g

1 Scrub or peel the carrots, and trim the ends.

2 Cook for 20 minutes. Drain, and process in a food processor.

3 Preheat the oven to 200°C/400°F/ Gas 6. Season the pureéd carrots well, and stir in the chopped coriander.

4 Beat the egg yolks into the carrot mixture until they are thoroughly mixed together.

5 In a separate bowl, whisk the egg whites until stiff.

6 Fold the egg whites into the carrot mixture and pour into four greased ramekins. Bake for about 20 minutes or until risen and golden. Serve immediately.

Pumpkin and Ham Frittata

A frittata is an Italian version of the Spanish tortilla, an omelette made from eggs and vegetables. Although they are sometimes eaten cold, this one tastes better warm or hot, served with crusty bread.

SERVES 4

30ml/2 tbsp sunflower oil
1 large onion, chopped
450g/1lb pumpkin, chopped into
    bitesize pieces
200ml/7fl oz/scant 1 cup chicken stock
115g/4oz/²⁄₃ cup chopped
    smoked ham
6 eggs
10ml/2 tsp chopped fresh marjoram
salt and ground black pepper

Nutritional information

Calories	231kcal/962kj
Fat	15.5g
Saturated fat	3.5g
Cholesterol	308mg
Fibre	1.8g

1 Preheat the oven to 190°C/375°F/ Gas 5. Oil a large shallow ovenproof dish. Heat the oil in a large frying pan and fry the onion for 3–4 minutes until it is softened.

2 Add the pumpkin and fry over a brisk heat for 3–4 minutes, stirring. Stir in the stock, cover and simmer over a gentle heat for 5–6 minutes until the pumpkin is slightly tender. Add the ham.

3 Pour the mixture into the prepared dish. Beat the eggs with the marjoram and a little seasoning. Pour into the dish and bake for 20–25 minutes until the frittata is firm and lightly golden.

Oatmeal Tartlets with Hummus

These wholesome little tartlets have a healthy base of oats rather than pastry, and are topped with a delicious mixture spiced with Middle Eastern flavours.

1 Preheat the oven to 160°C/325°F/ Gas 3. Mix together the oatmeal, bicarbonate of soda and salt in a large bowl. Rub in the butter until the mixture resembles fine crumbs. Stir in the egg yolk and add the milk if the mixture seems too dry.

2 Press into six 9cm/3½in tartlet tins (muffin pans). Bake for 25–30 minutes. Allow to cool.

3 Purée the chick-peas, the juice of one lemon, the fromage blanc and tahini in a food processor until smooth. Spoon into a bowl and season with black pepper and more lemon juice to taste. Stir in the chopped mint. Divide between the tartlet moulds, sprinkle with pumpkin seeds and dust with paprika.

SERVES 6

225g/8oz/2 cups medium oatmeal
2.5ml/½ tsp bicarbonate of soda
 (baking soda)
5ml/1 tsp salt
25g/1oz/2 tbsp butter
1 egg yolk
30ml/2 tbsp skimmed milk
400g/14oz can chick-peas, drained
 and rinsed
juice of 1–2 lemons
350g/12oz/1½ cups low-fat crème fraîche
60ml/4 tbsp tahini
45ml/3 tbsp chopped fresh mint
25g/1oz/2 tbsp pumpkin seeds
ground black pepper
paprika, for dusting

Nutritional information

Calories	365kcal/1532kj
Fat	16.8g
Saturated fat	2.9g
Cholesterol	35mg
Fibre	5.4g

Dill and Potato Cakes

Potato cakes are quite scrumptious and should be more widely made. Try this splendid combination and you are sure to be converted.

SERVES 10

225g/8oz/2 cups self-raising (self-rising) flour

45ml/3 tbsp butter, softened

pinch of salt

15ml/1 tbsp finely chopped fresh dill

175g/6oz/2 cups mashed potato, freshly made

30–45ml/2–3 tbsp milk, as required

1 Preheat the oven to 230°C/450°F/ Gas 8. Sift the flour into a bowl and add the butter, salt and dill. Mix in the mashed potato and enough milk to make a soft, pliable dough.

2 Roll out the dough on a well-floured surface until it is fairly thin. Cut into neat rounds with a 7.5cm/3in cutter.

3 Grease a baking sheet, place the cakes on it, and bake them for 20–25 minutes until risen and golden.

Nutritional information	
Calories	121kcal/510kj
Fat	4g
Saturated fat	0.8g
Cholesterol	0.4mg
Fibre	0.9

Wholemeal Herb Triangles

Stuffed with cooked chicken and salad, these make a good lunchtime snack and are also an ideal accompaniment to a bowl of steaming soup.

MAKES 8

225g/8oz/2 cups plain (all-purpose) wholemeal (whole-wheat) flour
115g/4oz/1 cup strong white bread flour
5ml/1 tsp salt
2.5ml/¹⁄₂ tsp bicarbonate of soda (baking soda)
5ml/1 tsp cream of tartar
2.5ml/¹⁄₂ tsp chilli powder
50g/2oz/¹⁄₄ cup soft margarine
60ml/4 tbsp chopped mixed fresh herbs
250ml/8fl oz/1 cup skimmed milk
15ml/1 tbsp sesame seeds

1 Preheat the oven to 200°C/400°F/ Gas 6. Lightly flour a baking sheet. Put the wholemeal flour in a mixing bowl. Sift in the remaining dry ingredients, including the chilli powder, then rub in the soft margarine.

3 Carefully cut the dough round into eight wedges, separate them slightly and bake for 15–20 minutes. Transfer to a wire rack to cool. Serve warm or cold.

Nutritional information	
Calories	222kcal/932kj
Fat	7.2g
Saturated fat	1.3g
Cholesterol	1.1mg
Fibre	3.5

2 Add the herbs and milk and mix quickly to a soft dough. Turn on to a lightly floured surface. Knead only very briefly or the dough will become tough. Roll out to a 23cm/9in round and place on the prepared baking sheet. Brush the triangles lightly with water and sprinkle evenly with the sesame seeds.

Variation

To make Sun-dried Tomato Triangles, replace the mixed fresh herbs with 30ml/2 tbsp drained chopped sun-dried tomatoes in oil and add 15ml/1 tbsp each mild paprika, chopped fresh parsley and chopped fresh marjoram.

Ham and Tomato Scones

These scones make an ideal accompaniment for soup. You can use wholemeal flour or a mixture of wholemeal and white flour for extra flavour, if you like.

SERVES 12

225g/8oz/2 cups self-raising (self-rising) flour
5ml/1 tsp dry mustard
5ml/1 tsp paprika, plus extra for sprinkling
2.5ml/½ tsp salt
25g/1oz/2 tbsp soft margarine
15ml/1 tbsp chopped fresh basil
50g/2oz/1 cup drained sun-dried tomatoes in oil, chopped
50g/2oz/⅓ cup chopped cooked ham
90–120ml/3–4fl oz/6 tbsp–½ cup skimmed milk, plus extra for brushing

Nutritional information

Calories	113kcal/474kj
Fat	4.2g
Saturated fat	0.7g
Cholesterol	3mg
Fibre	0.7g

1 Preheat the oven to 200°C/400°F/ Gas 6. Flour a large baking sheet. Sift the flour, mustard, paprika and salt into a bowl. Rub in the margarine until the mixture resembles crumbs.

Cook's Tip

To cut calories and fat, choose dry-packed sun-dried tomatoes and soak them in warm water.

2 Stir in the basil, sun-dried tomatoes and ham, and mix lightly. Pour in enough milk to mix to a soft dough.

3 Turn the dough out on to a lightly floured surface, knead briefly and roll out to a 20 x 15cm/8 x 6in rectangle. Cut into 5cm/2in squares and arrange on the baking sheet.

4 Brush lightly with milk, sprinkle with paprika and bake for about 12–15 minutes. Transfer to a wire rack to cool.

Cheese and Marjoram Scones

A guaranteed success at a hearty tea, these scones can also make a good basis for a light lunch, served with savoury toppings and a crunchy green salad.

1 Gently sift the two kinds of flour into a bowl and add the salt. Cut the butter into small pieces, and rub into the flour until it resembles fine crumbs.

2 Add the mustard, marjoram and grated cheese, and mix in sufficient milk to make a soft dough. Knead the dough lightly.

3 Preheat the oven to 220°C/425°F/ Gas 7. Roll out the dough on a floured surface to 2cm/³⁄₄in thickness and cut it out with a 5cm/2in square cutter. Grease baking trays with sunflower oil, and place the scones on the trays. Brush them with milk and sprinkle with the nuts. Bake for 12 minutes. Serve warm.

SERVES 18

115g/4oz/1 cup self-raising (self-rising) wholemeal (whole-wheat) flour
115g/4oz/1 cup self-raising (self-rising) flour
pinch of salt
40g/1¹⁄₂oz/3 tbsp butter
1.5ml/¹⁄₄ tsp dry mustard
10ml/2 tsp dried marjoram
50–75g/2–3oz/¹⁄₂–³⁄₄ cup finely grated Cheddar cheese
120ml/4fl oz/¹⁄₂ cup skimmed milk, or as required
5ml/1 tsp sunflower oil
50g/2oz/¹⁄₃ cup pecan nuts, chopped

Nutritional information	
Calories	90kcal/376kj
Fat	4.4g
Saturated fat	0.6g
Cholesterol	1mg
Fibre	0.5g

Chive and Potato Scones

These little scones should be fairly thin, soft in the middle and crisp on the outside.

SERVES 20

450g/1lb large potatoes
115g/4oz/1 cup plain (all-purpose)
  flour, sifted
30ml/2 tbsp olive oil
30ml/2 tbsp chopped chives
salt and ground black pepper
low-fat spread, for topping (optional)

Nutritional information

Calories	50kcal/211kj
Fat	1.2g
Saturated fat	0.2g
Cholesterol	0mg
Fibre	0.5g

1 Cook the potatoes in a pan of salted boiling water for 20 minutes, then drain thoroughly. Return the potatoes to the clean pan and mash them. Preheat a griddle over a low heat.

2 Add the flour, olive oil and chopped chives with a little salt and pepper to the hot mashed potatoes in the pan. Mix to a soft dough.

3 Roll out the dough on a well-floured surface to a thickness of 5mm/¼in and stamp out rounds with a 5cm/2in pastry (cookie) cutter.

4 Cook the scones, in batches, on the hot griddle or frying pan for about 10 minutes until they are golden brown on both sides. Keep the heat low. Top with a little low-fat spread, if you like, and serve immediately.

Cheese and Chive Scones

Try serving these savoury scones instead of bread rolls.

1 Preheat the oven to 200°C/400°F/ Gas 6. Sift the flours and salt into a mixing bowl, adding any bran left over from the flour in the sieve.

2 Crumble the feta cheese and rub into the dry ingredients. Stir in the chives, add the milk and mix to a soft dough.

3 Turn out on to a floured surface and knead lightly until smooth. Roll out to 2cm/³⁄₄in thick and stamp out nine scones with a 6cm/2¹⁄₂in biscuit (cookie) cutter.

4 Transfer the scones to a non-stick baking sheet. Brush with skimmed milk, then sprinkle over the cayenne pepper. Bake in the oven for 15 minutes, or until golden.

MAKES 9

115g/4oz/1 cup self-raising (self-rising) white flour
150g/5oz/1¹⁄₄ cup self-raising (self-rising) wholemeal (whole-wheat) flour
2.5ml/¹⁄₂ tsp salt
75g/3oz/¹⁄₃ cup feta cheese
15ml/1 tbsp chopped fresh chives
150ml/¹⁄₄ pint/²⁄₃ cup skimmed milk, plus extra for glazing
1.5ml/¹⁄₄ tsp cayenne pepper

Nutritional information

Calories	121kcal/507kj
Fat	2.2g
Saturated fat	1.1g
Cholesterol	0.4mg
Fibre	1.9g

Herb Popovers

Popovers are muffin-size batter puddings with a crisp brown crust and a delicious moist centre.

MAKES 12

3 eggs
250ml/8fl oz/1 cup skimmed milk
25g/1oz/2 tbsp butter, melted
75g/3oz/²⁄₃ cup plain
   (all-purpose) flour
0.75ml/⅛ tsp salt
1 small sprig each mixed fresh herbs,
   such as chives, tarragon, dill
   and parsley

Nutritional information	
Calories	75kcal/316kj
Fat	3.5g
Saturated fat	0.8g
Cholesterol	49mg
Fibre	0.3g

1 Preheat the oven to 220°C/425°F/ Gas 7. Grease 12 small ramekins or popover cups.

2 With an electric mixer, beat the eggs until blended. Beat in the milk and melted butter.

3 Sift together the flour and salt, then beat into the egg mixture to combine the ingredients thoroughly.

4 Strip the herb leaves from the stems and chop finely. Mix together and measure out 15ml/1 tbsp. Stir the herbs into the batter.

5 Pour batter into the cups until they are half-full, then bake for about 25 minutes. Do not open the oven door; the hot air will escape and the popovers will deflate. If you want drier popovers, pierce each with a skewer after baking and bake for another 5 minutes.

Cheese Popovers

Popovers are wonderful when flavoured with a strong, piquant cheese, such as Parmesan.

1 Preheat the oven to 220°C/425°F/ Gas 7. Grease 12 small ramekins or popover cups.

2 With an electric mixer, beat the eggs until blended. Beat in the milk and melted butter.

3 Sift together the flour, salt and paprika, then beat into the egg mixture. Add the cheese and stir.

4 Fill the prepared cups half-full and bake for 25–30 minutes, or until golden. Do not open the oven door during baking or the popovers may fall. For drier popovers, pierce each one with a knife after the 30 minutes baking time and bake for 5 minutes more. Serve hot.

Variation

To make Yorkshire Pudding Popovers as an accompaniment for roast beef, omit the cheese and use 4–6 tbsp of the pan drippings to replace the butter. Put them into the oven in time to serve warm with the beef.

MAKES 12

3 eggs
250ml/8fl oz/1 cup skimmed milk
30ml/2 tbsp butter, melted
75g/3oz/²⁄₃ cup plain
   (all-purpose) flour
1.5ml/¹⁄₄ tsp salt
1.5ml/¹⁄₄ tsp paprika
90ml/6 tbsp freshly grated
   Parmesan cheese

Nutritional information	
Calories	92kcal/387kj
Fat	4.8g
Saturated fat	1.6g
Cholesterol	52mg
Fibre	0.3g

Curry Crackers

These spicy, crisp little nibbles are very low in fat and are ideal for serving with drinks.

MAKES 12

50g/2oz/½ cup plain
(all-purpose) flour
1.5ml/¼ tsp salt
5ml/1 tsp curry powder
1.5ml/¼ tsp chilli powder
15ml/1 tbsp chopped fresh
coriander (cilantro)
30ml/2 tbsp water

Nutritional information

Calories	15kcal/65kj
Fat	0.1g
Saturated fat	0.01g
Cholesterol	0mg
Fibre	0.2g

1 Preheat the oven to 180°C/350°F/ Gas 4. Sift the flour and salt into a mixing bowl, then add the curry powder and chilli powder. Make a well in the centre and add the chopped fresh coriander and water. Gradually incorporate the flour and mix to a firm dough.

2 Turn on to a lightly floured surface, knead until smooth, then leave to rest for 5 minutes.

3 Cut the dough into 12 pieces and knead into small balls. Roll each ball out very thinly to a 10cm/4in round.

4 Arrange the rounds on two ungreased baking sheets, then bake for 15 minutes, turning over once during cooking. Cool on a wire rack.

Variation

Omit the curry and chilli powders and add 15ml/1 tbsp fennel, caraway, onion or mustard seeds.

Oatcakes

Try serving these oatcakes with reduced-fat hard cheeses, or top them with thick honey for breakfast.

SERVES 8

175g/6oz/1½ cups medium oatmeal,
    plus extra for sprinkling
2.5ml/½ tsp salt
pinch of bicarbonate of soda
    (baking soda)
15g/½ oz/1 tbsp butter
75ml/5 tbsp water

Nutritional information

Calories	102kcal/427kj
Fat	3.4g
Saturated fat	0.7g
Cholesterol	0.1mg
Fibre	1.5g

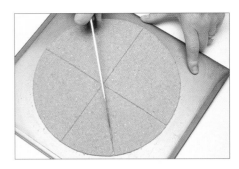

3 Turn the dough on to a surface sprinkled with oatmeal and knead to a smooth ball. Turn a large baking sheet upside down, grease it, sprinkle it lightly with oatmeal and place the ball of dough on top. Sprinkle the dough with oatmeal, then roll out to a 25cm/10in round.

4 Cut the round into eight equal sections, ease them apart slightly and bake for about 50–60 minutes until crisp. Leave to cool on the baking sheet, then remove the oatcakes using a metal spatula.

1 Preheat the oven to 150°C/300°F/ Gas 2. Mix the oatmeal with the salt and bicarbonate of soda in a bowl.

2 Melt the butter with the water in a small pan. Bring to the boil, then add to the oatmeal mixture and mix to a moist dough.

BREADS

There is nothing so appealing as the aroma of freshly baked bread and this selection is guaranteed to have your family asking for more. As well as some traditional favourites, there are tasty tempting recipes made with herbs, cheese and vegetables – and they are all low in fat!

French Bread

A fresh French stick is perfect to use to make garlic bread or sandwiches.

MAKES 2 LOAVES

10ml/2 tsp active dried yeast
475ml/16fl oz/2 cups lukewarm water
5ml/1 tsp salt
675–900g/1½–2lb/6–8 cups strong
   white bread flour
cornmeal, for sprinkling

1 Combine the yeast and water, stir, and leave for 15 minutes to dissolve. Stir in the salt.

2 Add the flour, 115g/4oz/1 cup at a time. Beat in with a wooden spoon, adding just enough flour for a smooth dough. Alternatively, use an electric mixer with a dough hook attachment.

3 Transfer to a floured surface and knead until smooth and elastic.

4 Shape into a ball, place in a greased bowl, and cover with a plastic bag. Leave to rise in a warm place until doubled in volume, for 2–4 hours.

Nutritional information	
Calories	96kcal/4111kj
Fat	0.4g
Saturated fat	0.1g
Cholesterol	0.mg
Fibre	0.9g

5 Transfer to a lightly floured board, halve the dough and shape into two long loaves. Place on a baking sheet sprinkled with cornmeal, and leave to rise for 5 minutes.

6 Score the tops in several places with a very sharp knife. Brush with water and place in a cold oven. Set a pan of boiling water on the bottom of the oven and set the oven to 200°C/400°F/Gas 6. Bake until crusty and golden, for about 40 minutes. Cool on a rack.

Cook's Tips

If you want a crisp, dark crust, spray the loaf with water during baking. Always preheat the oven; French bread (and all bread) requires a hot oven in order to rise completely.

White Bread

This classic white loaf is ideal for breakfast toast, or simply eaten warm from the oven.

MAKES 2 LOAVES

50ml/2fl oz/¼ cup lukewarm water
10ml/2 tsp active dried yeast
30ml/2 tbsp caster (superfine) sugar
475ml/16fl oz/2 cups lukewarm
   skimmed milk
30ml/2 tbsp butter or margarine
10ml/2 tsp salt
675–800g/1½–1¾lb/6–7 cups
   strong white bread flour

1 Combine the water, yeast and 15ml/ 1 tbsp sugar in a measuring cup and leave for 15 minutes.

2 Pour the milk into a large bowl. Add the remaining sugar, the butter or margarine, the salt and the yeast mixture.

3 Stir in the flour, 115g/4oz/1 cup at a time, until a stiff dough is formed. Alternatively, use a food processor.

4 Transfer the dough to a floured surface. To knead, push the dough away from you with the palm of your hand, then fold it toward you, and push it away again. Repeat until the dough is smooth and elastic.

5 Place the dough in a large greased bowl, cover with a plastic bag, and leave to rise in a warm place until doubled in volume, 2–3 hours. Grease two 23 x 13cm/9 x 5in loaf tins (pans).

6 Knock back (punch down) the risen dough with your fist and divide in half. Form into loaf shapes and place in the tins, seam-side down. Cover and leave to rise in a warm place until almost doubled in volume, about 45 minutes.

7 Preheat the oven to 190°C/375°F/ Gas 5. Bake for 45–50 minutes, until firm and brown. Unmould and tap the bottom of a loaf, if it sounds hollow, the loaf is done. If necessary, return to the oven and bake a few minutes more. Transfer to a rack to cool.

Nutritional information

Calories	178kcal/757kj
Fat	1.8g
Saturated fat	0.3g
Cholesterol	1mg
Fibre	1.4g

Onion Focaccia

This Italian flat bread may be topped with vegetables, cheese or herbs before being baked in the oven. Focaccia is related to pizza and is eaten as a snack. It is characterized by the dimples in the surface, which are created to hold a little olive oil and keep the bread moist.

MAKES 2

675/1½lb/6 cups strong white
    bread flour
2.5ml/½ tsp salt
2.5ml/½ tsp caster (superfine) sugar
15ml/1 tbsp easy-blend (rapid-rise)
    dried yeast
60ml/4 tbsp extra virgin olive oil
450ml/¾ pint/scant 2 cups
    hand-hot water

To finish

2 red onions, thinly sliced
45ml/3 tbsp extra virgin olive oil
15ml/1 tbsp coarse salt

1 Sift the flour, salt and sugar into a large bowl. Stir in the yeast, oil and water and mix to a dough using a round-bladed knife. (Add a little extra water if the dough is dry.)

2 Turn out on to a lightly floured surface and knead for about 10 minutes until smooth and elastic. Put the dough in a clean, lightly oiled bowl and cover with clear film (plastic wrap). Leave to rise in a warm place until doubled in bulk.

3 Place two 25cm/10in plain metal flan rings on baking sheets. Oil the sides of the rings and the baking sheets.

4 Preheat the oven to 200°C/400°F/ Gas 6. Halve the dough and roll each piece to a 25cm/10in round. Press into the tins, cover and leave for 30 minutes to rise.

5 Make deep holes, about 2.5cm/1in apart, in the dough. Cover and leave for a further 20 minutes.

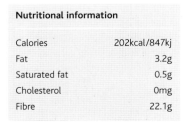

6 Scatter with the onions and drizzle over the oil. Sprinkle with the salt, then a little cold water, to stop a crust from forming.

7 Bake for about 25 minutes, sprinkling with water again during cooking. Cool on a wire rack.

Cook's Tip

Toppings for focaccia should be quite light. Try adding a mixture of basil, garlic and olive oil for a delicious Italian flavour. Chop the basil and garlic and blend with a little olive oil, season with salt and ground black pepper and spread over the focaccia, pushing the mixture into the dimples. Bake as usual. If you prefer rosemary, simply replace the basil with chopped rosemary and add a few small sprigs with a sprinkle of sea salt before baking. Serve with separate small bowls of balsamic vinegar and extra virgin olive oil.

Nutritional information

Calories	202kcal/847kj
Fat	3.2g
Saturated fat	0.5g
Cholesterol	0mg
Fibre	22.1g

Irish Soda Bread

If you want to make bread quickly, this recipe is perfect, because it does not need to rise. It is a great accompaniment to soup and cheese, or salad and pickles.

MAKES 1 LOAF

225g/8oz/2 cups plain
   (all-purpose) flour
225g/8oz/1 cup plain (all-purpose)
   wholemeal (whole-wheat) flour
5ml/1 tsp bicarbonate of soda
   (baking soda)
5ml/1 tsp salt
30ml/2 tbsp butter or margarine
350ml/12fl oz/1½ cups buttermilk
15ml/1 tbsp flour, for dusting

Nutritional information

Calories	188kcal/797kj
Fat	3.3g
Saturated fat	0.7g
Cholesterol	1mg
Fibre	2.3g

1 Preheat the oven to 200°C/400°F/ Gas 6. Grease a baking sheet.

2 Sift the flours, bicarbonate of soda and salt together in a bowl. Make a well in the centre and add the butter or margarine and buttermilk. Working outward from the centre, stir with a fork until a soft dough is formed.

3 With floured hands, gather the dough into a ball.

4 Transfer to a floured surface and knead for 3 minutes. Shape the dough into a large round.

5 Place on the baking sheet. Cut a cross in the top with a sharp knife.

6 Dust with flour. Bake until brown, for 40–50 minutes. Transfer to a wire rack to cool.

Brown Soda Bread

This is very easy to make – simply mix and bake. Instead of yeast, bicarbonate of soda and cream of tartar are the raising agents. This is an excellent recipe for those new to breadmaking.

MAKES 1 LOAF

450g/1lb/4 cups plain
    (all-purpose) flour
450g/1lb/4 cups plain (all-purpose)
    wholemeal (whole-wheat) flour
10ml/2 tsp salt
15ml/1 tbsp bicarbonate of soda
    (baking soda)
20ml/4 tsp cream of tartar (tartaric acid)
10ml/2 tsp caster sugar (superfine) sugar
50g/2oz/¼ cup butter
about 900ml/1½ pints/3¾ cups
        buttermilk or skimmed milk

1 Lightly grease a baking sheet. Preheat the oven to 190°C/375°F/Gas 5.

2 Sift all the dry ingredients into a large bowl, returning any bran from the flour back to the bowl.

3 Rub the butter into the flour mixture, then add enough buttermilk or milk to make a soft dough. You may not need all of it, so add it cautiously.

4 Knead the dough lightly until smooth – do not overknead – then transfer to the baking sheet and shape to a large round about 5cm/2in thick.

5 Using the floured handle of a wooden spoon, make a large cross on top of the dough. Sprinkle over a little extra wholemeal flour.

6 Bake for 40–50 minutes until well risen and firm. Cool for 5 minutes before transferring to a wire rack to cool down further.

Nutritional information	
Calories	185kcal/784kj
Fat	2.9g
Saturated fat	0.5g
Cholesterol	1.1mg
Fibre	2.8g

Austrian Three Grain Bread

A mixture of grains gives this close-textured bread a delightful nutty flavour.
Make two smaller twists, if preferred.

MAKES 1 LOAF

475ml/16fl oz/2 cups warm water
10ml/2 tsp active dried yeast
pinch of sugar
225g/8oz/2 cups strong white
    bread flour
7.5ml/1½ tsp salt
225g/8oz/2 cups malted brown flour
225g/8oz/2 cups rye flour
30ml/2 tbsp linseed
75g/3oz/¾ cup medium oatmeal
45ml/3 tbsp sunflower seeds
30ml/2 tbsp malt extract

Cook's Tip

Sunflower seeds and linseed add flavour,
vitamins, minerals and fibre to this bread
and are an important addition to healthy
eating. Whole grains can help to protect
against many common diseases such as
heart attacks, strokes and diabetes.

Variation

Vary the seeds in this recipe according to
what you have in the cupboard. Caraway
seeds, poppy seeds and sesame seeds
would all add a delicious flavour.

Nutritional information

Calories	367kcal/1540kj
Fat	5.4g
Saturated fat	0.6g
Cholesterol	0mg
Fibre	6.7g

1 Put half the water in a jug. Sprinkle
the yeast on top. Add the sugar, mix
well and leave for 10 minutes.

2 Sift the white flour and salt into a
mixing bowl and add the other flours.
Set aside 5ml/1 tsp of the linseed and
add the rest to the flour mixture with the
oatmeal and sunflower seeds. Make a
well in the centre. Add the yeast mixture
to the bowl with the malt extract and the
remaining water. Gradually incorporate
the flour.

3 Mix to a soft dough, adding extra
water if necessary. Turn out on to a
floured surface and knead for about
5 minutes until smooth and elastic.
Return to the clean bowl, cover with a
damp dishtowel and leave to rise for
about 2 hours until doubled in bulk.

4 Grease a baking sheet. Turn the
dough on to a floured surface, knead
for 2 minutes, then divide in half. Roll
each half into a 30cm/12in long sausage.

5 Twist the two sausages together,
dampen the ends and press to seal.
Lift the twist on to the prepared baking
sheet. Brush the plait with water, sprinkle
with the remaining linseed and cover
loosely with a large plastic bag (ballooning it to trap the air inside). Leave
in a warm place until well risen. Preheat
the oven to 220°C/425°F/Gas 7.

6 Bake the loaf for 10 minutes, then
lower the oven temperature to
200°C/400°F/Gas 6 and cook for about
20 minutes more, or until the loaf sounds
hollow when it is tapped underneath.
Transfer the bread to a wire rack and
leave to cool.

Anadama Bread

A delicious traditional American yeast bread flavoured with molasses.

1 Combine the yeast and lukewarm water, stir well, and leave for 15 minutes to dissolve.

2 Meanwhile, combine the cornmeal, butter or margarine, molasses and boiling water in a large bowl. Add the yeast, egg, and half of the flour. Stir together to blend.

3 Stir in the remaining flour and salt. When the dough becomes too stiff, stir with your hands until it comes away from the sides of the bowl. If it is too sticky, add more flour; if too stiff, add a little water.

4 Knead until smooth and elastic. Place in a bowl, cover with a plastic bag, and leave in a warm place until doubled in volume, for 2–3 hours.

5 Grease two 18 x 7.5cm/7in x 3in bread tins (pans). Knock back (punch down) the dough with your fist. Shape into two loaves and place in the tins, seam-side down. Cover and leave in a warm place until risen above the top of the tins, for 1–2 hours.

6 Preheat the oven to 190°C/375°F/Gas 5. Bake for 50 minutes. Remove and cool on a rack, or set across the tin to cool.

MAKES 2 LOAVES

10ml/2 tsp active dried yeast
60ml/4 tbsp lukewarm water
50g/2oz/½ cup cornmeal
40g/1½oz/3 tbsp butter
  or margarine
60ml/4 tbsp molasses
175ml/6fl oz/¾ cup boiling water
1 egg
350g/12oz/3 cups strong white
  bread flour
10ml/2 tsp salt

Nutritional information

Calories	146kcal/616kj
Fat	3.1g
Saturated fat	1.6g
Cholesterol	18.5mg
Fibre	0.9g

Squash Yeast Bread

The grated courgettes add an extra moistness to the texture of this tasty loaf.

1 In a colander, alternate layers of grated courgettes and salt. Leave for 30 minutes, then squeeze out the moisture with your hands.

2 Combine the yeast with 50ml/2fl oz/ ¼ cup of the lukewarm water, stir and leave for 15 minutes to dissolve the yeast.

3 Place the courgettes, yeast and flour in a bowl. Stir together and add just enough of the remaining water to obtain a rough dough.

4 Transfer to a floured surface and knead until smooth and elastic. Return the dough to the bowl, cover with a plastic bag, and leave to rise in a warm place until doubled in volume, for about 1½ hours.

5 Grease a baking sheet. Knock back (punch down) the risen dough with your fist and knead into a tapered cylinder. Place on the baking sheet, cover and leave to rise in a warm place until doubled in volume, for about 45 minutes.

6 Preheat the oven to 220°C/425°F/ Gas 7. Brush the bread with olive oil and bake for about 40–45 minutes, or until the loaf is a golden colour. Cool on a rack before serving.

MAKES 1 LOAF

450g/1lb/3½ cups courgettes (zucchini), grated
30ml/2 tbsp salt
10ml/2tsp active dried yeast
300ml/½ pint/1¼ cups lukewarm water
400g/14oz/3½ cups strong white bread flour

Nutritional information

Calories	191kcal/8111kj
Fat	1.2g
Saturated fat	0.2g
Cholesterol	0mg
Fibre	2g

Spinach and Bacon Bread

Use smoked lean back bacon for the best possible flavour with the minimum of fat for this tasty bread.
One loaf will give you eight portions, so it is a good idea to freeze one of the loaves.

MAKES 2 LOAVES

450ml/¾ pint/scant 2 cups
    warm water
10ml/2 tsp active dried yeast
pinch of sugar
15ml/1 tbsp olive oil
1 onion, chopped
115g/4oz smoked bacon rashers
    (strips), chopped
225g/8oz chopped spinach, thawed
    if frozen
675g/1½lb/6 cups strong white
    bread flour
7.5ml/1½ tsp salt
7.5ml/1½ tsp freshly grated nutmeg
25g/1oz/¼ cup grated reduced-fat
    Cheddar cheese

Cook's Tip

If using frozen spinach, be sure to squeeze
out any excess liquid or the resulting
dough will be too sticky.

Nutritional information

Calories	344kcal/1446kj
Fat	4.3g
Saturated fat	0.7g
Cholesterol	3.94mg
Fibre	3.36g

1 Put the water in a bowl. Sprinkle the yeast on top and add the sugar. Mix well and leave for 10 minutes. Lightly grease two 23cm/9in cake tins (pans).

2 Heat the oil in a frying pan and fry the onion and bacon for 10 minutes until golden brown. Meanwhile, if using frozen spinach, drain it thoroughly.

3 Sift the flour, salt and nutmeg into a mixing bowl and make a well in the centre. Add the yeast mixture. Tip in the fried bacon and onion (with the oil), then add the spinach. Gradually incorporate the flour mixture and mix to a soft dough.

4 Transfer the dough to a floured surface and knead for 5 minutes until smooth and elastic. Return to the clean bowl, cover with a damp dishtowel and leave in a warm place to rise for about 2 hours, until doubled in bulk.

5 Transfer the dough to a floured surface, knead briefly, then divide it in half. Shape each half into a ball, flatten slightly and place in a tin, pressing the dough so that it extends to the edges. Mark each loaf into eight wedges and sprinkle with the cheese. Cover loosely with a plastic bag and leave in a warm place until well risen. Preheat the oven to 200°C/400°F/Gas 6.

6 Bake the loaves for 25–30 minutes, or until they sound hollow when they are tapped underneath. Transfer to a wire rack to cool.

Prosciutto and Parmesan Bread

Served with a tomato and onion salad, this nourishing bread almost becomes a meal in itself. For a more subtle cheesy flavour, try Grana Padano instead of Parmesan cheese.

MAKES 1 LOAF

225g/8oz/2 cups self-raising (self-rising) wholemeal (whole-wheat) flour
225g/8oz/2 cups self-raising (self-rising) white flour
5ml/1 tsp baking powder
5ml/1 tsp salt
5ml/1 tsp black pepper
75g/3oz prosciutto
25g/1oz/⅓ cup freshly grated Parmesan cheese
30ml/2 tbsp chopped fresh parsley
45ml/3 tbsp Meaux mustard
350ml/12fl oz/1½ cups buttermilk
skimmed milk, to glaze

Nutritional information	
Calories	250kcal/1053kj
Fat	3.7g
Saturated fat	1.3g
Cholesterol	7.1mg
Fibre	3.8g

1 Preheat the oven to 200°C/400°F/Gas 6. Flour a baking sheet. Place the wholemeal flour in a bowl and sift in the white flour, baking powder and salt. Add the pepper and the prosciutto. Set aside about 15ml/1 tbsp of the grated Parmesan and stir the rest into the flour mixture with the parsley. Make a well in the centre.

2 Mix the mustard and buttermilk together, pour into the flour and quickly mix to a soft dough.

3 Transfer the dough to a floured surface and knead briefly. Shape into an oval loaf, brush with milk and sprinkle with the reserved Parmesan cheese. Put the loaf on the prepared baking sheet.

4 Bake the loaf for 25–30 minutes, or until it sounds hollow when tapped underneath. Cool on a wire rack.

Olive and Herb Bread

Olive breads are popular all over the Mediterranean. For this Greek recipe use rich oily olives or those marinated in herbs, rather than canned ones.

MAKES 2 LOAVES

2 red onions, thinly sliced
30ml/2 tbsp olive oil
225g/8oz/2 cups pitted black or
    green olives
800g/1¾lb/7 cups strong white
    bread flour
7.5ml/1½ tsp salt
20ml/4 tsp easy-blend (rapid-rise)
    dried yeast
45ml/3 tbsp roughly chopped parsley,
    coriander (cilantro) or mint
457ml/16fl oz/2 cups hand-hot water

1 Fry the onions in the oil until soft. Roughly chop the olives.

2 Put the flour, salt, yeast and parsley, coriander or mint in a large bowl with the olives and fried onions and pour in the water. Mix to a dough, adding a little more water if the mixture feels dry.

3 Transfer to a lightly floured surface and knead well for about 10 minutes.

4 Put in a clean bowl, cover with clear film (plastic wrap) and leave in a warm place until doubled in bulk.

5 Preheat the oven to 220°C/425°F/ Gas 7. Lightly grease two baking sheets. Turn the dough on to a floured surface and cut in half. Shape into two rounds and place on the baking sheets. Cover loosely with lightly oiled clear film and leave until doubled in size.

6 Slash the tops of the loaves with a knife, then bake for about 40 minutes or until the loaves sound hollow when tapped on the base. Transfer to a wire rack to cool.

Nutritional information	
Calories	157kcal/664kj
Fat	2.9g
Saturated fat	0.4g
Cholesterol	0mg
Fibre	1.8g

Variation

Shape the dough into 16 small rolls. Slash the tops as above and reduce the cooking time to 25 minutes.

Sun-dried Tomato Braid

This is a marvellous Mediterranean-flavoured bread to serve at a summer buffet or barbecue.

MAKES 1 LOAF

300ml/½ pint/1¼ cups warm water
5ml/1 tsp active dried yeast
pinch of sugar
225g/8oz/2 cups strong wholemeal (whole-wheat) bread flour
225g/8oz/2 cups strong white bread flour
5ml/1 tsp salt
1.5ml/¼ tsp freshly ground black pepper
50g/2oz/⅔ cup drained, chopped sun-dried tomatoes in oil, plus
15ml/1 tbsp oil from the jar
25g/1oz/⅓ cup freshly grated Parmesan cheese
30ml/2 tbsp red pesto
5ml/1 tsp coarse salt

Variation

If you are unable to locate red pesto, use 30ml/2 tbsp chopped fresh basil mixed with 15ml/1 tbsp sun-dried tomato purée (paste).

Nutritional information	
Calories	294kcal/1233kj
Fat	12.1g
Saturated fat	2.1g
Cholesterol	3.4mg
Fibre	3.4g

1 Put half the warm water in a jug. Sprinkle the yeast on top. Add the sugar, mix well and leave for 10 minutes.

2 Put the wholemeal flour in a mixing bowl. Sift in the white flour, salt and pepper. Make a well in the centre and add the yeast mixture, sun-dried tomatoes, oil, Parmesan, pesto and the remaining water. Gradually incorporate the flour and mix to a soft dough, adding a little extra water if necessary.

3 Transfer the dough to a floured surface and knead for 5 minutes until smooth and elastic. Return to the clean bowl, cover with a damp dishtowel and leave in a warm place to rise for about 2 hours until doubled in bulk. Lightly grease a baking sheet.

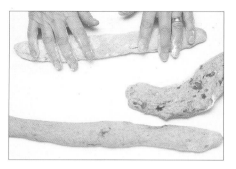

4 Transfer the dough on to a lightly floured surface and knead for a few minutes. Divide the dough into three equal pieces and shape each into a 30cm/12in long sausage.

5 Dampen the ends of the three sausages. Press them together at one end, braid them loosely, then press them together at the other end. Place on the baking sheet, cover and leave in a warm place for 30 minutes until well risen. Preheat the oven to 220°C/425°F/Gas 7.

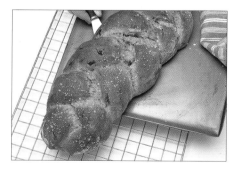

6 Sprinkle the braid with the coarse salt. Bake for 10 minutes, then lower the temperature to 200°C/400°F/Gas 6 and bake for a further 15–20 minutes, or until the loaf sounds hollow when tapped underneath. Cool on a wire rack.

Rosemary Bread

Sliced thinly, this herb bread is delicious when served with soup for a light meal.

MAKES 1 LOAF

- 7g/¼ oz easy-blend (rapid-rise) dried yeast
- 175g/6oz/1½ cups strong wholemeal (whole-wheat) bread flour
- 175g/6oz/1½ cups self-raising (self-rising) white flour
- 10ml/2 tsp butter, melted, plus extra for greasing
- 50ml/2fl oz/¼ cup warm water
- 250ml/8fl oz/1 cup skimmed milk
- 15ml/1 tbsp caster (superfine) sugar
- 5ml/1 tsp salt
- 15ml/1 tbsp sesame seeds
- 15ml/1 tbsp dried chopped onion
- 15ml/1 tbsp fresh rosemary leaves, plus extra to decorate
- 115g/4oz/1 cup cubed Cheddar cheese
- coarse salt

Nutritional information

Calories	188kcal/795kj
Fat	5.6g
Saturated fat	1.7g
Cholesterol	6mg
Fibre	2.2g

1 Mix the easy-blend dried yeast with the flours in a large mixing bowl. Add the melted butter. Stir in the warm water, milk, sugar, salt, sesame seeds, onion and rosemary. Knead thoroughly until quite smooth.

2 Flatten the dough, then add the cheese cubes. Quickly knead them in until they are well combined.

3 Place the dough in a large clean bowl greased with a little butter, turning it so that it becomes lightly greased on all sides. Cover with a clean, dry cloth. Put the greased bowl and dough in a warm place for about 1½ hours, or until the dough has risen and doubled in size.

4 Grease a 23 x 13cm/9 x 5in loaf tin (pan) with the remaining butter. Knock back (punch down) the dough to remove some of the air, and shape it into a loaf. Put the loaf into the tin, cover with the clean cloth used earlier and leave for about 1 hour until it has doubled in size once again. Preheat the oven to 190°C/375°F/Gas 5.

5 Bake for 30 minutes. During the last 5–10 minutes of baking, cover the loaf with foil to prevent it from becoming too dark. Remove from the loaf tin and leave to cool on a wire rack. Decorate with rosemary leaves and coarse salt scattered on top.

Spiral Herb Bread

An attractive and nutritious bread that is ideal for serving with a salad for a healthy lunch.

MAKES 2 LOAVES

425g/15oz/3⅔ cups strong white
    bread flour
15ml/1 tbsp salt
30ml/2 tbsp easy-blend (rapid-rise)
    dried yeast
550ml/18fl oz/2½ cups lukewarm water
25g/1oz/2 tbsp sunflower margarine
large bunch of parsley, finely chopped
bunch of spring onions (scallions), chopped
garlic clove, finely chopped
salt and ground black pepper
1 egg, lightly beaten

1 Combine the flour, salt and yeast in a large bowl. Make a well in the centre and pour in the water. With a wooden spoon, stir from the centre, working outward to obtain a rough dough.

2 Transfer the dough to a floured surface and knead until smooth and elastic. Return to the bowl, cover with a plastic bag, and leave for about 2 hours, until doubled in volume.

3 Meanwhile, combine the margarine, parsley, spring onions and garlic in a large frying pan. Cook over a low heat, stirring until softened. Season with salt and pepper and set aside.

4 Grease two 23 x 13cm/9 x 5in loaf tins (pans). When the dough has risen, cut in half and roll each half into a rectangle about 35 x 23cm/14 x 9in. Brush both with the beaten egg. Divide the herb mixture between the two, spreading just up to the edges.

5 Roll up each half of dough to completely enclose the filling and pinch the short ends to seal. Place in the tins, seam-side down. Cover the dough with a clean dishtowel and leave undisturbed in a warm place until the dough has risen above the rim of the tins.

6 Preheat the oven to 190°C/375°F/ Gas 5. Brush the loaves with milk and bake for about 55 minutes, until the bottoms sound hollow when tapped. Transfer to a wire rack and leave the loaf to stand until cool.

Nutritional information

Calories	85kcal/356kj
Fat	1.2g
Saturated fat	0.5g
Cholesterol	7.2mg
Fibre	1.5g

Buttermilk Graham Bread

Graham flour is slightly coarser than most flours, but wholemeal flour will make equally delicious bread. If you don't have sesame seeds, use poppy seeds or caraway seeds.

MAKES 8

10ml/2 tsp active dried yeast
120ml/4fl oz/½ cup lukewarm water
225g/8oz/2 cups graham or strong
   wholemeal (whole-wheat) bread flour
350g/12oz/3 cups strong white bread flour
130g/4½oz/generous 1 cup cornmeal
10ml/2 tsp salt
30ml/2 tbsp caster (superfine) sugar
50g/2oz/¼ cup butter
475ml/16fl oz/2 cups
   lukewarm buttermilk
1 beaten egg, for glazing
sesame seeds, for sprinkling

Nutritional information

Calories	195kcal/824kj
Fat	4g
Saturated fat	0.8g
Cholesterol	10mg
Fibre	1.9g

1 Combine the yeast and water, stir, and leave for 15 minutes to dissolve.

2 Mix together the graham or wholemeal flour, white flour, cornmeal, salt and sugar in a large bowl. Make a well in the centre of the dry ingredients and pour in the yeast mixture, then add the butter and the buttermilk.

3 Stir from the centre, mixing in the flour until a rough dough is formed. If the mixture is too stiff, use your hands.

4 Transfer to a floured surface and knead until smooth. Place in a clean bowl, cover, and leave in a warm place until doubled, for 2–3 hours.

5 Grease two 20cm/8in square baking tins (pans). Knock back (punch down) the dough. Divide into eight equal pieces and roll the pieces into balls. Place four balls in each tin. Cover and leave in a warm place until the dough rises above the rim of the tins, about 1 hour.

6 Preheat the oven to 190°C/375°F/ Gas 5. Brush with the glaze, then sprinkle over the sesame seeds. Bake for about 40 minutes, or until the bottoms sound hollow when tapped. Leave to cool on a wire rack.

Naan

There are various recipes for making naan, but this one is particularly easy to follow. Always serve naan warm, preferably straight from the grill, or wrap them in foil until you are ready to serve the meal.

MAKES 6

5ml/1 tsp caster (superfine) sugar
5ml/1 tsp active dried yeast
150ml/¼ pint/⅔ cup lukewarm water
225g/8oz/2 cups strong white bread flour
5ml/1 tsp ghee or butter
5ml/1 tsp salt
50g/2oz/¼ cup low-fat
   margarine, melted
5ml/1 tsp poppy seeds

1 Put the sugar and yeast in a small bowl, add the warm water and mix well until the yeast has dissolved. Leave for 10 minutes or until the mixture becomes frothy.

2 Place the flour in a large mixing bowl, make a well in the middle and add the ghee or butter, and salt, then pour in the yeast mixture.

3 Mix well, using your hands, to make a dough, adding some more water if the dough is too dry. Turn out on to a floured surface and knead for about 5 minutes or until smooth.

4 Place the dough back in the clean bowl, cover with foil and leave to rise in a warm place for 1½ hours or until doubled in size.

Nutritional information

Calories	177kcal/744kj
Fat	5.1g
Saturated fat	1.2g
Cholesterol	0.5mg
Fibre	0.2g

5 Preheat the grill (broiler) to very hot. Transfer the dough to a floured surface and knead for a further 2 minutes. Break off small balls with your hand and roll into rounds about 12cm/4½in in diameter and 1cm/½in thick.

6 Place on a sheet of greased foil and grill (broil) for 7–10 minutes, turning twice to brush with margarine and sprinkle with poppy seeds.

Poppy Seed Rolls

Pile these soft rolls in a basket and serve them for breakfast or with dinner. If you prefer, you could make one large plaited or braided loaf instead of rolls.

MAKES 12

300ml/½ pint/1¼ cups warm
    skimmed milk
5ml/1 tsp active dried yeast
pinch of sugar
450g/1lb/4 cups strong white
    bread flour
5ml/1 tsp salt
1 egg

For the topping
1 egg, beaten
poppy seeds

Cook's Tip

Use easy-blend (rapid rise) dried yeast if you prefer. Add it directly to the dry ingredients and mix with hand-hot milk. The rolls will require only one rising (see package instructions). Vary the toppings; linseed, sesame seeds and caraway seeds are all suitable. Try adding caraway seeds to the dough, too, for extra flavour.

Nutritional information

Calories	160kcal/674kj
Fat	2.4g
Saturated fat	0.5g
Cholesterol	32.6mg
Fibre	1.2g

1 Put half the warm milk in a small bowl. Sprinkle the yeast on top. Add the sugar, mix well and leave to stand for 30 minutes.

2 Sift the flour and salt into a mixing bowl. Make a well in the centre and pour in the yeast mixture and the egg. Gradually incorporate the flour, adding enough of the remaining milk to mix to a soft dough.

3 Turn the dough on to a floured surface and knead for 5 minutes until smooth and elastic. Return to the clean bowl, cover with a damp dishtowel and leave in a warm place to rise for about 1 hour until doubled in bulk.

4 Lightly grease two baking sheets. Turn the dough on to a floured surface. Knead for 2 minutes, then cut into 12 pieces and shape into a variety of rolls.

5 Place the rolls on the prepared baking sheets, cover loosely with a large plastic bag (ballooning it to trap the air inside) and leave to stand in a warm place until the rolls have risen well. Preheat the oven to 220°C/425°F/Gas 7.

6 Glaze the rolls with the beaten egg, sprinkle with poppy seeds and bake for 12–15 minutes until golden brown. Transfer to a wire rack to cool.

Index

Amaretto cake, nectarine, 60
Anadama bread, 146
angel cake, 57
apples: apple and pear skillet cake, 61
apple couscous pudding, 33
apple-sauce bread, 89
baked apple in honey and lemon, 38
spiced apple cake, 53
apple, apricot and walnut
loaf, 85
apricots: nut loaf, 97
apricot sponge bars, 76
apricot yogurt cookies, 77
filo and apricot purses, 30
glazed apricot sponge, 45
Austrian three-grain bread, 144

banana: and apricot Chelsea buns, 70
banana and cardamom bread, 82
banana and ginger teabread, 86
banana and gingerbread slices, 54
banana orange loaf, 84
glazed banana spice loaf, 87
baked blackberry cheese cake, 36
blueberry and orange baskets, 26
blueberry streusel slice, 74
brown soda bread, 143
buttermilk graham bread, 156

calzone, 111
cardamom and saffron tealoaf, 104
carrots:
carrot soufflés, 122
celeriac gratin, 121
cheese: and chive scones, 131
cheese and marjoram scones, 129
cheese popovers, 133
prosciutto and Parmesan bread, 150
chestnut and orange roulade, 16
chive and potato scones, 130
chocolate:
chocolate and orange angel cake, 62
chocolate banana cake, 64
Christmas cake, eggless, 56
coffee
coffee sponge drops, 50
Tia Maria gâteau, 66
cranberry orange bread, 90
curry crackers, 134

dates: date and nut malt loaf, 93
date-nut bread, 98
sticky date and apple bars, 75
dill and potato cakes, 126
dried fruit loaf, 92

Easter bread, Greek, 106
equipment, 8–9

feather-light peach pudding, 47
filo and apricot purses, 30
filo scrunchies, 31
French bread, 138
fruity bread pudding, 46

ginger:
ginger cake with spiced cream, 52
ginger upside-down pudding, 41
gooseberry crumble, crunchy, 40
Greek Easter bread, 106

ham and tomato scones, 128
herb pizza, fresh, 112
herb popovers, 132

Irish soda bread, 142

lemon walnut bread, 96
lining tins, 12

malt loaf, 94
date and nut malt loaf, 93
mango and amaretti strudel, 34
measuring techniques, 13
mini pizzas, 113
mixed berry tart, 24
muesli slice, chewy fruit, 73
muscovado meringues, 19

naan, 157
nectarine Amaretto cake, 60

oats:
oatcakes, 135
oatmeal tartlets with hummus, 125
oaty crisps, 78
olive and herb bread, 151
onion focaccia, 140
oranges:
orange cookies, 79
orange honey bread, 88
orange wheat loaf, 107

peaches: feather-light peach pudding, 47
latticed peaches, 42
peach roll, 58
pear and sultana teabread, 91
pepper, red and watercress filo parcels, 118
plums
hot plum batter, 44
plum filo pockets, 32

popovers:
cheese, 133
herb, 132
poppy seed rolls, 158
potatoes:
chive and potato scones, 130
dill and potato cakes, 126
prunes
prune and peel rock buns, 72
prune bread, 99
pumpkin and ham frittata, 124

raisin bread, 102
raspberry vacherin, 20
rosemary bread, 154

salmon parcels, 116
smoked salmon pizzettes, 110
snowballs, 18
spinach:
spinach and bacon bread, 148
spinach and cheese pie, 120
spinach and feta triangles, 114
spiral herb bread, 155
squash yeast bread, 147
strawberries
strawberry and apple
crumble, 39
strawberry gâteau, 22
sun-dried tomato braid, 152
Swedish fruit bread, 100
sweet potato and raisin bread, 103
sweet sesame loaf, 105

Tia Maria gâteau, 66
tomato cheese tarts, 117

vacherin, raspberry, 20

white bread, 139
wholemeal herb triangles, 127